OUR CONCERN
WITH THE THEOLOGY OF CRISIS

OUR CONCERN WITH THE THEOLOGY OF CRISIS

THE FUNDAMENTAL ASPECTS OF THE DIALECTICAL
THEOLOGY ASSOCIATED WITH THE NAME
OF KARL BARTH

APPRECIATIVELY PRESENTED AS OUR POSSIBLE
THEOLOGY WITH THE QUERY

WHETHER IT BE NOT OUR ONLY POSITIVE POSSIBILITY

*The crisis of Society and of the Church understood
as the crisis of the individual before God.*

By

WALTER LOWRIE, D.D.

The BOHLEN LECTURES for 1932

WIPF & STOCK · Eugene, Oregon

Wipf and Stock Publishers
199 W 8th Ave, Suite 3
Eugene, OR 97401

Our Concern with the Theology of Crisis
The Bohlen Lectures for 1932
By Lowrie, Walter
ISBN 13: 978-1-5326-0471-3
Publication date 8/5/2016
Previously published by Meador Publishing Company, 1932

DEDICATED
TO
G. A. A.
WITH FILIAL OBSERVANCE

PREFACE
TABLE OF CONTENTS
AND BIBLIOGRAPHY

THE JOHN BOHLEN LECTURESHIP

By the will of John Bohlen, deceased on the 26th day of April, 1874, the Rector, Church Wardens, and Vestrymen of the Church of the Holy Trinity, Philadelpiha, received in trust the sum of ten thousand dollars for the endowment of a lectureship upon the following terms and conditions:

"The money shall be invested in good substantial and safe securities and held in trust for a fund to be called The John Bohlen Lectureship, and the income shall be applied annually to a qualified person, whether clergyman or layman, for the delivery and publication of at least one hundred copies of two or more lecture sermons. These lectures shall be delivered at such time and place, in the city of Philadelphia, as the persons nominated to appoint the lecturer shall from time to time determine, giving at least six months' notice to the person appointed to deliver the same when the same may conveniently be done, and in no case selecting the same person as lecturer a second time within a period of five years. The payment shall be made to said lecturer, after the lectures have been printed and received by the trustees, of all the income derived from said fund, after defraying the cost of printing the lectrues and the other incidental expenses attending the same.

"The subject of such lectures shall be such as is within the terms set forth in the will of the Rev. John Bampton, for the delivery of what are known as the 'Bampton Lectures', at Oxford, or any other subject distinctly connected with or related to the Christian religion.

"The lecturer shall be appointed annually in the month of May, or as soon thereafter as can conveniently be done, by the persons who for the time being shall hold the offices of Bishop of the Protestant Episcopal Church of the Diocese in which is the Church of the Holy Trinity; the Rector of said Church; the Professor of Biblical Learning, the Professor of Systematic Divinity, and the Professor of Ecclesiastical History, in the Divinity School of the Protestant Episcopal Church in Philadelphia. In case either of said offices are vacant, the others may nominate the lecturer."

Under this trust the Rev. Walter Lowrie, D.D., was appointed to deliver the lectures for the year 1932.

PREFACE

This book has gradually been beaten into shape, as the result of conferences with students and professors in several seminaries and with a group of clergymen at the College of Preachers at Washington Cathedral. The first six lectures were delivered in Philadelphia on the Bohlen Foundation during May of this year. The last two were added to make the course more complete as it was delivered to the "School of the Prophets" held at Kanuga Lake, N. C., in July of this same year.

These lectures—and this book—are intended only for those who are inclined to feel a "concern" for the present crisis of Society and of the Church. The aim is missed if the hearer or reader retains the aloof attitude of a spectator, and does not come to realize that the crisis is his personal concern, the crisis of the individual.

No apology is necessary for *lecturing* on a subject of such serious concern as the Theology of Crisis; but if the terms of the Bohlen bequest did not require that these lectures be published, I might have hesitated to decide whether another *book* were needed to satisfy the curiosity of the public by describing this theology. That has already been done by five writers during the last four years.[1] I have no notion of doing over again

---

[1] H. Emil Brunner: *The Theology of Crisis,* 1929. R. Birch Hoyle: *The Teaching of Karl Barth,* 1930. Wilhelm Pauck: *Karl Barth,* 1931. J. Arundel Chapman: *The Theology of Karl Barth,* 1931. John McConnochie: *The Significance of Karl Barth,* 1931.

what on the whole has been so well done. Emil Brunner[2] has hardly done more than give a sample of his own theology. And, strangely enough, Hoyle, though he entitles his book *The Teaching of Karl Barth*, quotes chiefly from Brunner. Consequently Brunner has been made to loom too large in our view of the School of Crisis. Of Barth's writings, unfortunately, we have nothing in English except a collection of addresses entitled *The Word of God and the Word of Man*, and a popular address called *The Way of Life*. It is deplorable that none of his important works have yet been translated into English. The general curiosity about the imposing movement which he started would seem to be enough to embolden publishers to produce his works for English readers—especially his commentary on the Epistle to the *Romans*, which made his fame, and the first volume of his *Dogmatics*, entitled *Teaching about the Word of God*, which is his most considerate utterance.[3] All the books that have been written about Barth cannot be regarded as a substitute for Barth himself, and as interpretations they fail to accomplish all they aim at if the readers are unable to turn to the sources which are recommended to them.

What we need above all, however, is that some of us, aware of our crisis and taught to understand it, should write in the spirit of the Critical Theology and in a language understanded of our people.[4] When I

---

[2] Also in a later book entitled *The Word of God and the World*, 1931.
[3] I have been told that the Oxford University Press is about to publish an English translation of Barth's commentary on the Epistle to the Romans and that the Edinburgh University Press will publish a translation of his Dogmatics.
[4] *Tell John* is such a book, recently written by two English clergymen, Geoffry Allen and Roy McKay.

wrote my *Jesus according to St. Mark*[5] I was more influenced by Barth's *Romans* than I was then aware, and when I wrote *Religion or Faith*[6] I was fully conscious that it was a Barthian book. In both books it was the Barthian themes which were most generally reprobated or misunderstood. I conclude from this that a general interpretation of the principles of the Barthian theology is necessary to prepare the way for writers who are bold enough to speak this new language.

In the brief space at my disposal I cannot say so much as has been said by other English interpreters of Barth. Yet in a sense I say more, for I do not confine my attention to Karl Barth but am interested in the School of Crisis as a whole, and also in a larger school which has the same dominant interests, many of which can be traced to the influence of that tremendous Dane, Sören Kierkegaard, who failed to make any impression upon his own century and has become the predominant intellectual factor in ours. One might speak of the School of Kierkegaard, were it not that in it we must include writers so disparate as Ibsen the playwright, Barth the theologian, Heidegger the philosopher and Unamuno the novelist. Barth traces his intellectual lineage back to Kierkegaard, but beyond him to the Reformers, whereas Unamuno, who in his *Tragic Sense of Life* shows that he was no less powerfully influenced by Kierkegaard, exhibits the Catholic reaction to this influence. Kierkegaard and his school is far too large a theme for this little book, but I refer to it as a way of economizing space, because it reveals a principle of unity and serves to determine the points which are most deserving of attention.

---

[5] Longmans 1929.
[6] Marshall Jones 1930.

It is not merely lack of space which compels me to dwell exclusively upon the most important features of the Barthian theology and to detect as it were the greatest common denominator of the Barthian School and the schools closely related to it. And it is not a mediating tendency I follow, though I wish to ingratiate the reader's interest and to win his sympathy for the Theology of Crisis. I am inclined to dwell exclusively upon the points which "find me," assuming that they will make a like appeal to others. These are in fact the most salient points, and as such they are the most repellant features of the Barthian theology, yet at the same time they are the most attractive. I would not make them seem unnecessarily offensive, and because some are estranged from Barth by the suspicion that his reverence for the Bible is extravagant, I prefer to quote on this subject Bultmann (an authentic member of the School) who as a Biblical critic is notoriously radical. There is marked diversity among the individuals who compose the School of Crisis, and when we have discovered their greatest common denominator it is found to be common ground to several distinguished scholars who for one reason or another decline to adhere to the school of Barth or are even regarded as opponents. I am thinking especially of Paul Tillich, who frankly acknowledges the debt he owes to Barth, but goes his own way. And of Karl Heim, who is Barth's most eminent rival, and yet shares with him many of his profoundest convictions. To us in America, in the chaos to which theology has been reduced, the differences between such men are not nearly so obvious as the resemblances. They would make one school here, whereas in Germany, owing to the traditional rivalries of university life, they make several. The challenge of Karl Barth (especially the first shock produced by the second edition of the *Romans*) has profoundly affected the younger generation of theologians in Germany, so that the German Liberalism which has long been predominant in America is no longer dominant in the land of its origin. The plight of the Church in Germany is as bad as it is here, and more manifestly so. But at least there are in Germany leaders of thought who (to use Barth's phrase) are no longer content to deal with "absolute relatives and relative absolutes" and are intent upon distinguishing the categories. Living lately in Italy, I thought it significant that the Roman Church was watching with alert attention (through its Biblical Institute) every development of the Barthian movement—watching it with anxiety as a threat of the revival of Protestantism, yet not without a certain sympathy in recognition of the fact that as a return to the theology of the Reformation it is an approach, at least within speaking distance, to the classical theology of the middle ages. Barth is an appreciative student of St. Thomas, and he has confessed that, if he were shut up to a choice between Protestant Modernism and Catholicism, he would prefer to become a Catholic.

There is another sense in which I aim to say more than other interpreters of the Barthian theology have attempted to say. While no single book can tell *all* there is to tell about the Dialectical Theology (to use Barth's favorite title), I am bold enough to believe that in small compass I can state the *whole* of it. Above everything else I try to make its wholeness apparent. I am not unmindful of the fact that Barth repudiates the notion that his theology can be presented as a system. I understand that attitude and sympathize with it. But to seek after a principle of unity—the unifying principle which actually holds such a school together—is a very different matter.

Barth himself has furnished the clue to that search, pointing to a saying of Kierkegaard's as the principle which informs his whole thought. Discovering such a principle and applying it with due caution and diligence, every man can make his own Barthian theology.

WALTER LOWRIE.

Princeton, September 1932.

TABLE OF CONTENTS

LECTURE I

Introductory

	PAGE
Sören Kierkegaard	24
Popular Christianity	28
Doubts and queries about it	31
Barth's Protest	37
What is dogmatics	38
A Positive Protest	41
The dialectical method	42
Examples from Kierkegaard	46
Either-Or	49
Germany and here	50
Barth and Orthodoxy	53
Liberalism encounters Radicalism	54

LECTURE II

The Telos

The Problem of Time

A central principle	57
Its validity argued	59

The Telos

The difficulty of eschatology	66

CONTENTS

Barth an eschatologist 67
Death, Resurrection and the End 70
Quotation from Barth on 1 Cor. 15 72

LECTURE III

THE KAIROS

The Arche

The Beginning and the End 83
A definite direction 86

Between Two Worlds

The area of life and thought 89
Time qualified by the End 92
The Crisis 96
Contemporaneousness of Christ 97
Contemporaneousness of God's Word 98
The Kairos Group 100
Kierkegaard 100
Dynamic and authority of preaching 102
A parable of Kierkegaard's 104

LECTURE IV

GOD

God as the Crisis 109
"Meaning" and "Value" 110
"God is God" 111
The "distance" 112
From Barth's *Romans* 114
Mysticism 117
Religious experience 120

Revelation in Nature? 122
The transcendent God 123
Quotation from Brunner 127

LECTURE V

JESUS CHRIST

A dialectical term 131
Undialectically treated 132
The Calcedonian formula 136
Quotation from Barth 138
The Lord Jesus Christ 140
From Barth's *Romans* 142
"The historical Jesus" 144
"The humanity of Christ" 144
Quotation from Gogarten 148
The Mediator 151

LECTURE VI

REVELATION

A question of actuality 153
Faith 155
Kierkegaard, on how to read 157
The doctrine of revelation 162
Revelation or religion 165
Christian experience 167
The "I" and "Thou" relationship 168
Irrationalism 169
Christ as the Word 171
Not an historical force 174
Quotation from Bultmann 176

LECTURE VII

SALVATION

Themes necessarily omitted	185
Sin, Repentence, Faith, Justification	187
Law and religion	190
"Sanctification"?	196
Relative goodness, irrelevant	199
The distinction of Christianity	201

LECTURE VIII

PREACHERS AND PREACHING

A conspicuous topic	205
An act of daring	206
The Word of God is speech and act	209
The duty of preaching God's Word	211
The sermon as founded on the Bible	212
"Reminding people"	214

BIBLIOGRAPHY

Max Strauch, *Die Theologie Karl Barths*, Kaiser, München.
Emil Brunner, *The Theology of Crisis*, Scribners, 1929.
R. Birch Hoyle, *The Teaching of Karl Barth*, 1930.
Wilhelm Pauck, *Karl Barth*, Harpers, 1931.
John McConnachie, *The Significance of Karl Barth*, Hodder & Stoughton, 1931.
Zerbe, *The Karl Barth Theology*, Cleveland, 1931.
Adolf Keller, *Der Weg der dialectischen Theologie durch die kirchliche Welt*, Kaiser, München, 1931.

By KARL BARTH. Published by Kaiser, München.

Der Römerbrief. 1st ed. 1918. 2nd ed. (much enlarged) 1921.
Das Wort Gottes und die Theologie, 1924. Translated by Douglas Horton, with the title, *The Word of God and the Word of Man*, Hodder & Stoughton, 1928.
Die Auferstehung der Toten, a commentary on 1 Cor. 15, 1924.
Komm Schöpfer Geist (sermons, in part by Thurneysen), 1924.
Dogmatik, I. Prolegomena: Die Lehre vom Worte Gottes, 1927.
Erklärung des Philipperbriefs, 1928.
Suchet Gott so werdet Ihr leben (sermons), 1928.
Zur Lehre vom Heiligen Geist, 1930.
Vom Christlichen Leben (an address), 1926. Published in English by the Christian Student Movement, with the title *The Christian Life*, 1930.
Die Tehologie und die Kirche (collected addresses), 1928.

By EMIL BRUNNER. Published by Mohr, Tübingen.

Erlebnis, Erkentnis und Glaube, 1921.
Die Grenzen der Humanität, 1922.
Das Symbolische in der religiöse Erkentnis, 1923.
Die Mystik und das Wort, 1924.
Philosophie und Offenbarung, 1925.
Religionsphilosophie und Theologie, 1927.
Der Mittler, 1927.
The Word and the World, Scribners, 1931.

By FRIEDERICH GOGARTEN. Published by Diederich, Jena.

Von Glaube und Offenbarung, 1923.
Die religiöse Entscheidung, 1924.
Illusionen, 1926.

Ich glaube an den dreieinigen Gott, 1926.
Glaube und Wirklichkeit, 1928.
Die Schuld der Kirche gegen die Welt, 1930.
Wider die Aechtung der Autorität, 1930.

Edward Thurneysen, *Dostojewski*, 3rd ed. 1925. Besides his sermons mentioned above in connection with Barth, most of his writings are to be found in *Zwischen den Zeiten*, the bimonthly organ of the School of Crisis, now in its tenth year. In the files of this review many of the important writings of the school are to be found.

Rudolph Bultmann, *Jesus*, Deutsche Bibliothek, Berlin, 1929.
————, *Der Begriff der Offenbarung in NT*, Mohr, Tübingen, 1929.

Paul Tillich, *Die religiöse Lage der Gegenwart*, Ullstein, Berlin, 1926.
————, *Kairos* (the 1st Kairos Book, with contributions from the Kairos-Kreise), Reichl, Darmstatt, 1928.
————, *Protestantismus als Kritik und Gestaltung* (the 2nd Kairos Book), same publisher, 1929.
————, *Religöse Verwirklichung*, Furche-Verlag, Berlin, 1930.
————, *Kirche und Kultur*, Mohr, Tübingen, 1924.
————, *Das Dämonische*, Mohr, Tübingen, 1926.

Miguel De Unamuno, *Del sentimiento tragico della vida*, 4th ed. Renacimiento (Madrid, Barcelona, Buenos Aires), 1931. Translated into English by Flitch, with the title *The Tragic Sense of Life*, MacMillan, 1931.
Miguel De Unamuno, *L'Agonie du Christianisme*, Rieder, Paris, 1926.

Karl Heim, *The New Divine Order*, Christian Student Movement, London, 1930.
————, *Glaube und Denken*, Furche-Verlag, Berlin, 1931.
Martin Buber, *Ich und Du*, Insel-Verlag, Leipzig, 1923.

SÖREN KIERKEGAARD

Collected Works of Sören Kierkegaard, translated into German by Christoph Schrempf with the assistance of several scholars, and published by Dieterich in Jena.

(The date in brackets is that of the publication in Copenhagen.)

1 and 2. *Entweder—Oder*, 2 vol. (1843), 1922.
3. *Furcht und Zittern* (1843), 1923.
4. *Stadien auf dem Lebensweg* (1845), 1922.
5. *Der Begriff der Angst*, 2 vol. (1844), 1923.
6. *Philosophische Broken etc.* (1844), 1925.
7. *Unwissenschaftliche Nachricht* (1844), 1925.
8. *Die Krankheit zum Tode* (1849), 1924.

9. *Einübung im Christentum* (1850), 1924.
10. *Der Gesichtspunkt für meine Wirksamkeit als Schriftsteller* (1859), 1924.
11. *Zur Selbstprüfung der Gegenwart anbefohlen* (1851), 1922.
12. *Der Augenblick* (1855), 1923.

ERBAULICHE REDEN

1. *Sittlich-religiose Reden*, 1924.
2. *Erbauliche Reden in verschiedenen Geist*, 1924.
3. *Leben und Walten der Liebe*, 1924.
4. *Reden von 1848-1855*, 1924.

Translated by Theodor Haecker and published by Brenner Verlag, Innsbruck.

Der Pfahl im Fleisch, 1922.
Die Krisis und eine Krisis im Leben einer Schauspielerin, 1922.
Die Tagebücher, 2 vols. (1834-1855), 1923.
Der Begriff der Auserwälten, 1926.
Am Fusse des Altars.

Religiose Reden, translated by Haecker but published by Wiechmann, München, 1922.

Die Reinheit des Herzens, translated by Lina Geismar, Kaiser, München, 2nd ed. 1926.
Die Begriff der Ironie, translated by Kütemeyer, Kaiser, München, 1929.
There were earlier translations (11 vols. in all) not listed here.

In English.

Selections from Sören Kierkegaard, translated by Hollander and published as University of Texas Bulletin No. 2326, in 1923.

Books about Kierkegaard in German.

Bärthold, *Sören Kierkegaard*, Halberstadt, 1873.
―――――, *Noten zur S.K's Lebensgeschichte*, Halle, 1876.
―――――, *S.K's Personlichkeit*, Gütersloh, 1886.
G. Brandes, *Sören Kierkegaard*, Leipzig, 1879.
Bohlin, *Sören Kierkegaards Leben und Werden*, Gütersloh, 1927.
―――――, *Kierkegaards dogmatische Anschauung*, Gütersloh, 1927.
Diem, *Philosophie und Christentum bei Sören Kierkegaard*, München, 1929.
Geismar, *Sören Kierkegaard, seine Lebensentwichlung, etc.*, Gottingen, 1927.
Gilg, *Sören Kierkegaard*, München, 1926.
Haecker, *Sören Kierkegaard und die Philosophie der Innerlichkeit*, Innsbruck, 1923.

——————, *Der Begriff der Wahrheit bei S.K.*, Innsbruck, 1932.
Hoffmann, *S.K. und die religiose Gewissheit*, Göttingen, 1910.
Himmelstrup, *Sören Kierkegaards Sokratesauffassung*, Neumünster, 1927.
Hirsch, *Kierkegaard-Studien*, in 3 parts.
Künneth, *Die Lehre von der Sünde, etc.* Gütersloh, 1927.
Monrad, *Sören Kierkegaard, sein Leben und seine Werke*, Jena, 1909.
Niedermeyer, *Sören Kierkegaard und die Romantik*, Leipzig, 1914.
Przwara, *Das Geheimnis Kierkegaards*, München, 1929.
Ruttenbeck, *Der Christliche Denker und seiner Werke*, Berlin, 1929.
Thust, *Sören Kierkegaard der Dichter des Religiosen*, München, 1931.
Van Höffding, *Sören Kierkegaard*, Stuttgart, 1922.
Vetter, *Frömmigkeit als Leidenschaft, eine Deutung Kierkegaards*, Leipzig, 1928.
Voigt, *Sören Kierkegaard im Kampfe mit der Romantik*, Berlin, 1928.
Münch, *Philosophie S.K's*, Leipzig, 1902.
——————, *Relative absoluta?* Leipzig, 1903.
Reuter, *K's Religionsphilosophische Gedanken*, Leipzig, 1914.
Regine Schlegel (übers. von Meyer), *Sien Verhältnis zu "ihr"*, Stuttgart, 1905.

I have listed here 56 volumes published in German and one in English. It is significant to note that 45 of them have been published within the last decade. But I do not pretend that this list of German works is complete. I have set down only those which I have been able to obtain for my library. I could list at least as many articles which have appeared in German reviews. There are likely many publications of this current year which have not yet been brought to my attention. I have made no attempt to gather the works which have been published in Danish or in the other Scandinavian languages which I cannot read, nor even those which have been published in French, Italian and Spanish. The German list suffices to show how immense has become the momentum of the Kierkegaard revival on the Continent of Europe and with how quick a tempo it has superseded the interest which before the war was concentrated upon Nietzsche. George Brandes' well-known essay on the literary art of Kierkegaard first brought his name to the attention of the European public. Ibsen's *Brand* was written under Kierkegaard's influence, though we were hardly aware of that until now. Unamuno's interest in Kierkegaard has prompted South American publishers to begin the translation of his works. North America is as backward as England. Tardily I see a small book by F. W. Fulford on S. K. privately printed in Oxford without date but not before 1908. I am well aware that in this place the imperfect bibliography which I have ventured to insert here is a manifest intrusion. In publishing it I call attention to our shame and summon those who are competent to do so to make amends for it. The only amend now possible to me is this accusing bibliography. But for what reason have we so many universities? Is it to insure that studious youth shall be shielded from all contacts with contemporary thought?

OUR CONCERN
WITH THE THEOLOGY OF CRISIS

Our Concern With the Theology of Crisis

LECTURE I

INTRODUCTORY

I call this chapter "Introductory"; but by that title I would not prompt you to adopt a supine attitude, patiently expecting to hear only preliminary observations. Preliminary observations about Barth and other members of his school, about his religious pilgrimage and the writings which register his attainment, about Kierkegaard, Dostoiewski and others through whom he traces his spiritual lineage, and about the philosophical and theological situation in Germany which is the background against which you must view his work—all this you may need to hear, if you have not read any of the numerous introductions to Barthianism. But obviously, in these few lectures, we have no time for so slow an approach. Whatever of this sort imperatively needs to be said, must be interjected incidentally in the course of the discussion. The purely preliminary matter I can eliminate without regret because I am not intent upon describing with the detachment of an historian all the phases of Barthian theology which actually are observable and which are relevant to the German environment; but rather am I desirous of determining the character it must assume in our environment, if it is to be assimilated at all. I desire first of all to make you feel the need of it, and then the necessity. "Necessity," when it is understood as absolute, leaves us no longer in the attitude of a spectator, enquiring if it be possible or impossible. The alternative, Christian or not Christian? signifies, Life or death? I might say ever so much about the Theology of Crisis, and yet be saying nothing to the point, if I were not seeking first of all to make you recognize it as your crisis. If I do not present it as a crisis, I am not presenting it at all. For that is the essence of it. Of all that Barth derived from Kierkegaard, that which became most central to his thinking was the crisis involved in the absolute alternative, "Either—Or"—the solemn choice which is presented to us, not once for all, but again and again, and sometimes in circumstances so trivial that we can easily ignore its eternal significance. Under the same influence, and as his rendering of the same thought, Ibsen puts into the mouth of his hero Brand the motto, "All or Nothing." Unamuno rightly interprets this as the alternative of life or death, and like Kierkegaard he dwells upon the "anguish" of man in the face of this dilemma. Martin Heidegger, the philosopher now most acclaimed in Germany, generalizes Kierkegaard's "Idea of Anguish" to make it serve (under the name of *Sorge*—care) as explanation of the substance of all created being. Under the influence of Kierkegaard his ontology reflects the Biblical scheme of man's fall and redemption. The individual is "gefallen an das Man" (*i.e.* lost in the opinions of the impersonal generality), and to become himself again (or indeed for the first time) he must make the critical "Decision."[1] In accepting the invitation to deliver these lectures I proposed to devote them to either of two themes: Karl Barth, or Sören Kierkegaard. The latter is evidently our greater need, but it is still an unfelt want—a long unfelt want, which perhaps must be filled before it is felt. Kierkegaard's influence, as I have hinted, is not only deep but wide. Very properly we might speak of his School. We must recognize that it *comprises* the School of Barth, that it has as good a claim to be called the School of Crisis, and no less appropriately might be called a School of Dialectical Theology. This consideration justifies me in considering here, along with Barth, remoter members of the School of Kierkegaard. It may even serve as an excuse for

---

[1] Having remarked upon the immense influence of Sören Kierkegaard upon some of the most significant leaders of modern thought, it may be necessary to remind you that he was a litterateur, aesthetic critic, a philosopher, a psychologist, a moralist, a theologian and an anticlerical who flourished (ironical word!) in Denmark about the middle of the last century, till, overwhelmed by the ridicule of the people and the obduracy of the clergy, he died in his forty-second year as he was carrying home the last money he had in the bank. His influence began to be felt in Europe soon after the beginning of this century, when his works were being translated one by one into German. Barth gave great impetus to this vogue. And now all of his published works are to be had in German, as well as some of his private papers, making twenty volumes in all—"a literature within a literature," as Kierkegaard liked to say of his work—and about it has grown up a literature of comment which is equal in volume. In English, we insular people (I refer especially to this continent of North America) have nothing of Kierkegaard's except a brochure containing *Selections* translated by S. M. Hollander, published as a Bulletin of the University of Texas, No. 2326, in date of July 8, 1923; and we have no comment upon him that I know of except an article by Swansen in the Philosophical Review which appraises him merely as a philosopher. The South American continent is less insular. I am told that three of Kierkegaard's works have been translated into Spanish and published in the Argentine Republic. The book by Unamuno which I have referred to is entitled *Del sentimiento tragico de la vida*. It is to be had also in English, *The Tragic Sense of Life*.

quoting appreciatively many a word of Nietzsche's, who, because of a striking similarity of mind, has been called "a pagan Kierkegaard." Barth generously acknowledges his debt to Kierkegaard; but how immense it is, and how pervading, from first to last, one will not understand without reading this master.

This that I have been saying may appear to be preliminary, and I shall linger upon it no longer. For I am in haste to introduce you *into* the Theology of Crisis. In this lecture we shall plunge deeply into it.

But before we start straight for the goal I require you (like carrier pigeons when they are released) to circle around in order to discover where we are at (to use a strong though vulgar idiom) and get the right orientation. That is to say, I ask you now to consider what actually are the doctrines most surely believed among us and most widely acceptable. And to fix your reflection upon this query I presume to propose a common creed. I express it persuasively, as a preacher would do with the aim of winning the assent of his hearers—or I had better say, of winning their approbation, since I am assuming that already all have been converted to these doctrines.

If in what I am about to say you detect a note of irony, you ought not to resent it in this place, for it is an example of the method followed by Barth and Kierkegaard. From Socrates Kierkegaard learned not only dialectic but irony. And if it seem presumptuous of me to assume that a creed which I compose might serve as a common creed for Protestant Christendom—and then to presume to criticise it in every detail—you are to understand that I do not do this superciliously. There is hardly an article of this creed which does not represent my belief at one time or another during the last forty-two years since I matriculated as a student of theology. Who among

POPULAR CHRISTIANITY

us has escaped the influence of the nineteenth century? I reflect grimly that the creed of Lausanne or that of the great missionary conference at Jerusalem would have served the present purpose almost as well—if I did not shrink from criticising in the name of Barth documents which are accounted so sacred. It is a matter of course that any creed which depends today upon the suffrages of a representative gathering of Protestants must at least be vaguely enough expressed to admit of a Modernist interpretation.

(1) Of all the religions of mankind, Christianity, we are sure, is the highest; (2) for we regard it as the climax of a long evolutionary process, (3) in which the people of Israel, because they were a race especially gifted for religion, played a conspicuous part, while above this high level of human attainment towered (4) the Founder of our religion, (5) a religious genius so unique that men may well hesitate to deny that (6) in some sense he was divine. (7) We acclaim him as the Master, in appreciation of the fact that his (8) religious consciousness, as manifested in precept and example, is in some degree normative for us—in spite of the fact that the movement to which he gave (9) impetus has resulted in clearer conceptions of the divine and of the human than was possible at the beginning. We still envisage the moral task in the figurative terms which Jesus proposed, as a (10) "building up of the kingdom of God," which we understand as (11) the realization of a perfect human society, having no doubt that (12) man is equal to such a task, (13) because man is inherently a child of God and therefore essentially good. We cannot ignore the fact that this great end is (14) more remote than Jesus seems to have conceived, and that the chief obstacle is something that used to be called sin. But we are confident that (15) at the long

last the evolutionary process will eliminate (16) this organic defect of our brute inheritance. And if ever we reflect how great a dose of resignation is required of us in laboring for a utopia in which we shall personally have no part, we are consoled by the Christian belief in (17) the immortality of the soul, which we associate with the "kingdom of heaven." (18) By this faith in the continuity of the here and the hereafter, of time and eternity, we have (19) robbed death of its terror, and even of its apparent significance. Jesus purified religion by teaching us to see (20) that God is our Father, and therefore can be approached without fear and without the sense of aweful distance. (21) For God is essentially near, immanent in his world, and therefore discoverable in it—(22) but especially in the depths of the human heart, in a more or less mystical experience. (23) Experience is therefore the foundation of faith, (24) though Jesus of Nazareth as an historical person, in whom we see realized the (25) ideal of humanity, is none the less necessary to give a note of (26) authority to our intuitions. (27) Therein lies the supreme value of the Gospels. But a unique religious value attaches to the whole Bible: to the (28) Old Testament, because it is a record of the most significant evolution of the religious idea (what may be called by analogy the vertebrate line of development); and (29) to the New Testament, because it is the record of the experience of the first generations of Christians, which we cannot but regard as the classical experience, (30) since the disciples who in line were nearest to the initial thrust must have experienced it more vividly, though they naturally could not understand its significance so adequately as we who view it from a position immensely more remote.

In this creed I count thirty fundamental propositions. Though perhaps not all of them are expressed as one or another of you would prefer, I believe it would be difficult to formulate a creed which today would be more generally acceptable in Protestant Christendom. If such be the fact, it will seem as if I were adopting the clumsiest and most uningratiating way of recommending the Barthian Theology when I say that it asserts the polar opposite of all this which we most surely believe—that it can be summarily understood as the contradiction, point by point, of all of our thirty propositions. That, you may judge, is enough to condemn it without a further hearing. But pray suspend this judgment while you reflect that this creed, if it indeed be our creed, is precisely the faith which confessedly we have so much difficulty in maintaining and recommending, which encounters so many objections, and is assailed by so many doubts. We might be grateful, I should suppose, to anyone who would rid us of the weak perplexities that have so long baffled us—even if at the same time he confronts us with new and sterner difficulties. With you I might argue—assuming that the majority will confess to being Pragmatists—that our present creed cannot be true, seeing that at this present time it notoriously does not "work," is evidently *not* "the faith which overcometh the world."

Be patient with me while I recite the creed again—incorporating with it now the doubts and queries which the preacher might be supposed to pencil upon the margin of his manuscript, though he would not propound them to the congregation he is seeking to edify.

(1) Religion! Who can altogether disguise from himself what a questionable thing it is? Especially if one is familiar with the innumerable religions of mankind, from the basest to the highest, and reflects

at times upon the quality of his own religiousness. "Human—all-to-human!" And if Christianity could be shown to be supreme in *this* category, how infinitely far *that* is from its absolute claim to be "the Way"! (2) Christianity as the climax of evolution would have seemed a flat anticlimax to the men of the Bible, to whom the Word of God was as fire from heaven. (3) The very "relative absoluteness" of *our* claim is demonstrated when we derive it from the religious genius of the Hebrews. Quite apart from the fact that this alleged genius for religion seems exceedingly questionable when we consider what the Prophets said about this people, what their historians relate, and what the religious depravity of the Semitic peoples most nearly akin to them lead us to surmise. (4) It may not occur to the preacher to question the propriety of speaking of Jesus as the Founder of our religion, unless he has read Christoph Blumhardt's indignant repudiation of this title; (5) but it is clear that we have an elegant instance of "absolute relativism" in the attempt to base the unique claim of Jesus to be the Christ upon the observation that as a religious genius he surpassed even the Prophets of his gifted race. (6) When we assert that for this reason he should be regarded as divine, we mean (at the most) that he was a man who *became* God. (7) When we call Jesus "the Master," the people may be satisfied with the ambiguity of the title, and because of its use in the Gospels it may seem to them to be justified. But we preachers know that it means nothing else but *rabbi*, and unambiguously implies that we value Jesus most of all for his teaching, and that we need only *that* to enable us to save ourselves. The title by which he was known "in the days of his flesh" —in the time of his incognito, as Kierkegaard and Barth like to say—was no longer appropriate when by his resurrection from the dead he was made known as both Lord and Christ. From that moment until our day the Church never spoke of him as *rabbi, didaskalos, magister,* or teacher, but as *Mara, Kyrios, Dominus,* Lord. When we say "Master" it is an ominous indication of a change of faith. (8) We cannot speak of the "religious consciousness" of Jesus as the source of his inspiration without putting him altogether on a level with ourselves. For man has been defined as a religious animal—"incurably religious." It is much more significant that Jesus, religious man as he was, was so irreligious as the Evangelists take pains to represent him. (9) We unconsciously desert the standpoint from which we have viewed Jesus as a teacher when, using a physical analogy, we represent his influence upon history in terms of cause and effect. Although at this point the preacher is not likely to note any caveat on the margin, the Barthians here register an indignant protest. (10) The preacher will still continue to exhort his people to coöperate in "building up the kingdom of God," and to add pathos to the appeal he may remind them that "God has no hands but our hands"; yet he himself knows (or is in a position to learn) that the Scripture nowhere implies that man is expected to build, or to help to build the Kingdom of God. (11) And that this kingdom is equivalent to social reform, culture, civilization, progress, which is a notion we learned from Ritschl, we can now no longer teach with a good conscience, seeing that even such scholars as do not understand it eschatologically are agreed that Jesus had in mind no secular interests when he proclaimed the coming of the kingdom of God. The kingdom simply "comes," and man "enters" it ... or fails to enter.

But to listen to more of this (to nineteen more

queries and doubts and denials!) would be tedious to the hearer, and only for the sake of the reader (who can skip if he will), and to show completely the fragility of our creed, do I continue to register the doubts which assail us point by point.

(12) That man is equal to the task of realizing even the ideal of a perfect human society is an illusion which no people in Europe has shared with us since the war, and which we hardly can hold any longer with steady conviction. (13) That man is essentially good (or even "too good to be damned," as Dr. Holmes ironically put it) can be believed only with heroic obstinacy. Jesus "knew what is in man," and no one has given a more somber account of "the things that proceed out of the heart of man" (Mark 7:21-23). Nietzsche, with his indignant cry that "man is a thing which must be surpassed," echoes the complaint of the ancient Prophets—and the glad expectation of the Apostles of our Lord. (14) We cannot without grave disquietude reflect upon the fact that this kingdom which seemed "near" to Jesus seems still very far away to us . . . after two thousand years. (15) And though it is natural for us to think of the development of the "kingdom" in evolutionary terms, it is plain that the men of the Bible were acquainted with no such category. (16) For that same reason, if for no other, they could not explain sin away as a vestigial defect or a mere "not yet." (17) When we come to the doctrine of the immortality of the soul, it may be presumed that the preacher will know enough philosophy to write on the margin the significant name "Plato!" But will he know enough about the Bible to recognize that this is *not* a Scriptural doctrine? and that it is *not* equivalent to the "resurrection of the dead"? (18) Or that it *could* have no place in the Scriptures for the reason that

the men of the Bible did not at all share our notion of continuity as between this world and the next, between time and eternity. (19) We all, like good Christian Scientists, skim triumphantly over the grim fact of death, and do not like to hear anyone speak of corpses, or coffins, or biers, or graves, or burials. It is not in the *Monitor* alone we read of a man who has "passed" and whose "rites" will be held. "Crucified, dead and buried," is the tremendous lapidary formula of the Apostles' Creed! To the men of the Bible, because of their realism, death was too awe-full a fact to be slurred over; and it was most tremendous to the men of the New Testament because of the faith (or shall we call it "the beautiful risk"?) that beyond that brink was Life! "Where there are no graves there are no resurrections," is a saying of Nietzsche's. Wherefore St. John does not think of hiding from us how Jesus was moved at the tomb of Lazarus, and the other Evangelists do not scruple to let us see the shuddering horror with which he faced his own death. This has often been compared with the serenity of Socrates; and those who do not know that death, "the last enemy," is more significant to the Christian, than to other men may think that Jesus did not meet his end like a "Christian." But death is significant also with reference to this present life of which it is the end. It is not, as we like to think, merely an event which some day we shall encounter; but because it is the only event we can certainly count on, it defines what we *are* in every moment. And this perception is not distinctive of Evangelical piety: it is sober common sense, such as we find in the Epicurean Ecclesiastes, and commonly among the Greeks, who by the picture of a human skeleton illustrated the Delphic saying adopted by Socrates, "Know thyself." To one who will deign to take notice of death it is at once *tremendum* and *fascinans*—to use Otto's expressions. "What after all is the *numinous*," says Bultmann, "but death itself?" In refusing to notice it we drive madly by a divine signal which is meant to save our life— God's signal, Stop!

(20) That Jesus brought God nearer to us, in teaching us to call him Father, is truth—but it is true only when we hold it in dialectical tension with the other truth that God is infinitely exalted. We must not for a moment forget that he is the "Father *in heaven*." Even the Son addressed him as "Holy Father," and holiness means at least "distance"— "unapproachable and full of Glory." Jesus, we may say in dialectical terms is "the nearness in that distance" (I use an expression of Barth's). But even in the nearness of Jesus we must recognize the distance. (21) Today nothing is so much taken for granted as God's *immanence* in the world which he has created —the absolute nearness of the Creator—and the belief that he is clearly discoverable in the things which he has made. And yet the preacher might be moved to write a *Caveat!* on the margin of this proposition, if he reflects that precisely here is the field where the fearful battle is waged between science and religion.

Against the remaining propositions of our creed (items 22 to 30) I should expect to see no marginal notes or queries. For with regard to the value of religious experience (and the "Christian experience" most of all) we are as yet troubled by no doubts. We have all become Methodists—without our knowing it we have all become disciples of Schleiermacher, "the father of modern theology." The notion that upon individual experience is founded the faith of the individual, that upon collective experience is founded the theology of the Church, that the Gospels reflect the religious experience of Jesus, and that the New Testament as a whole derives its authority solely from the fact that it registers the experience of the first generation of Christians—all these positions are now common to Liberals, Anglo-Catholics and Evangelicals. It is notorious that the mystic finds God (and all that he needs to know about him) in the depths of his own consciousness (or unconsciousness)—and how many more there are who believe they could find him there, if only they cared to take the pains! This is the only place where our creed seems unshaken and unshakable. Therefore it is at this place Barth and his School (who are not inclined to punch the air or break down open doors) enter their most vigorous protest. By the same token, this is the place where you will be most inclined to resent their protest.— Unless you have already been led to consider in what jeopardy we put the faith when we found it upon experience, and how helplessly we have delivered ourselves into the hands of the psychologists.

In this tedious enumeration I have mentioned most of our favorite beliefs and many of the Barthian protests against them. Barthian protests, and yet not *distinctively* Barthian; for anyone could make them, and many had been making them, point by point—but querulously, as doubts, and without perceiving any wholeness in the protest. Therefore they had not the power, nor even the intention, to overthrow: they merely undermined, but *that* they did thoroughly. Here is the naturalistic explanation of the fact that these so solid seeming walls of Jericho fell down flat at the first blast of Barth's trumpet. The foundations had already disintegrated. The significant thing is that Barth did not tap the wall suspiciously here and there, but made men perceive the wholeness of his protest, almost before he was aware of it himself. He made us perceive that in every article of our creed—in our exaltation of religion, of Christian experience, of mysticism, of the kingdom of God as a social Utopia, and of Jesus as the ideal of humanity —we were not thinking of God but of man. Not long ago an anonymous clerical writer in the *Atlantic Monthly* bewailed the fact that the preacher is no longer able to pronounce the name of God in a way that arouses a feeling of the numinous, a sense of aweful reverence. Barth explains this when he calls our attention to the fact that while we thought we were speaking about God we were merely "saying Man with a loud voice." We could not ignore this, as we had ignored the querimonious doubts of this man or the other about our creed; for in this we heard a resolute "No!" God's "No!" A divine and salutory signal to *stop!*

At the first, while he was writing his *Romans*, Barth conceived that he was doing nothing more than write marginal notes—but "marginal notes to *all* theology." He saw the distinction of his theology in the fact that it was a "corrective." And this point of view he does not relinquish even now when he is writing his *"Dogmatics,"* which he does not presume to call a theology, still less a systematic theology. Very significant is the fact that over the Introduction to this work he writes this inscription:

WHAT WE CALL DOGMATICS IS PAINSTAKING EFFORT AFTER THE KNOWLEDGE OF THE LEGITIMATE CONTENT OF CHRISTIAN DISCOURSE ABOUT GOD AND MAN.

In the first paragraph he makes plain what that means.

"There is such a thing as Christian dogmatics because there is such a thing as Christian speech. There was Christian speech before there was Christian dogmatics, and when there is no more Christian speech, then no more Christian dogmatics. Dogmatics is an explicit concern about Christian speech, which existed before dogmatics, and apart from it still occurs. This is not, as in homiletics, a concern about its rhetorical effectiveness; and not, as in apologetics, concern about its inherent power to convince the hearers by reason of its appropriateness to their ways of thinking and feeling; but simply and only a concern about the *legitimacy* of its contents—one might also say the suitableness of its contents, meaning the inward suitableness, suitableness in relation to that about which Christian speech speaks. That is assuredly a subject about which questions can be raised. There is not only such a thing as perfect and less perfect Christian speech, not only inherently evident and less evident; there is also speech which is legitimate and illegitimate, real and unreal, speech which serves the truth and speech which serves error, edifying and destructive speech. There is no Christian speech, whether it be uttered in the name of the Church or of the individual, which does not have to meet the test of this question about the legitimacy of its content. And this question is the question of dogmatics. Because this question is justified, there has always been, since first there was Christian speech, such a thing (though not exactly with this name) as Christian dogmatics, concern with regard to the knowledge of the legitimate content of Christian speech. And because this question will be justified so long as there are Christian speakers, just so long must dogmatics follow Christian speech like its shadow—as a reminder that even Christian speech is not spoken from heaven but on earth. Dogmatics does not inspire Christian speech. It does not create its content or even its form. It simply assumes it as a fact, form and content and all. But wherever without its assistance Christian discourse is held, it asks whether and in how far, with reference to the point at issue, all is well and wisely said. It seeks a universally valid answer to the question, under what conditions one *could* wisely speak about God. When we say Christian speech we naturally do not mean all and every sort of speech that Christians might use, but particular speech about that which makes Christians Christian, about the Christianly understood relationship betweeen God and man. Dogmatics rests upon the assumption that this speech is by no means infallibly released, but rather that in this matter truth and error are to be distinguished, right and wrong, legitimate and illegitimate, real and unreal. It rests upon the assumption that *criticism* and the query about a *norm* applicable to the phenomenon of Christian speech is not only permissible but is required by the very nature of this phenomenon. It therefore does not measure Christian speech by a rule that is foreign to its nature. But it confronts it with its own measuring rod, reminds it of its own immanent logic, it discovers what this speech evidently means, what it must mean if it understands itself aright, when it really would be what it is called, namely, Christian speech. At least it seeks to do all this, is painstaking about it. For dogmatics after all, like the Christian speech which it examines, is human and not divine. Yet human task as it is, it proceeds upon the assumption that Christian speech can and must be taken seriously, taken at its word, that even in its human illegitimacy it at least aims at a legitimate content, that reality (within the bounds of the humanly possible) is even in this field an attainable and a necessary aim, and that it is worth while, where Christian discourse is held, to take pains to insure that it shall be Christianly spoken."

This passage shows that Barth, though he speaks now in more measured terms as a theological professor, is still chiefly concerned with theology as a corrective, so that even his dogmatics is predominantly critical and polemical, and never in the strictest sense systematic. But this, as we shall see later, is only what we must expect of the Dialectical Theology, if it is to remain truly dialectical.

The quotation I have made is longer than it need be to prove that point. But it is significant in other respects, and I am glad to introduce it here because it relieves me for a moment of the necessity of describing Barthianism in my own terms. You will understand that this necessity means the necessity of being brief. I would linger a moment here to remark that this definition of dogmatics is well calculated to persuade those who are inclined to slight theology that it is an exceedingly necessary discipline, even though it is a long unfelt want which it fills. And never more necessary than in our day and place, seeing that the speech of our preachers is now hardly tempered by self-criticism, and is chastened by no effective criticism from without.

It is natural that, in the first shock of surprise which was occasioned by Barth's *Romans,* his attitude should have been thought to be predominantly negative. Speaking of himself at that time he says that he was like a man groping his way in the dark up the winding stair of a belfry and snatching for support at a rope—which to his dismay proved to be the bell-rope. He was as much astonished as anyone else at the unexpected clanging of the church bell. Commenting on this figure, I would remark upon the significance of the fact that it was the *church* bell that rang so unexpectedly. It reminded men how far they had wandered from the Church, without meaning to, and without knowing it. The familiar sound of the church bell—though they had not heard it for so long a time—carried associations of authority, and also of comfort. For that reason Barth's protest was perceived to be not merely negative. That is to say, Barth's protest would not have been truly heard at all, if it had been heard merely as his all-too-human protest against the human errors of the current theology, and not heard also as God's "No." And God's "No" men cannot bear to hear, if they do not hear in it also God's "Yes."

In the light of this context I say again that all the queries and doubts I so tediously enumerated a while ago, though substantially they are such criticisms as Barth has made, do not yet give us an idea what Barthianism is as a whole, and cannot even be said to be a part of it. For this reason first of all, that they are expressions of doubt and not of faith. For I am assuming that the marginal notes of the average preacher are question marks attached to his own sermon, are consequently only doubts about his faith, and are not in the proper sense of the word negations. A strong negation, a round No, is always supported by some faith. And it is proper to apply here St. Paul's saying, "Whatsoever is not of faith is sin." In Barth's protest, because it was an absolute negation, the divine "No" was heard—and in it the divine "Yes" was audible as a reminiscence of the old theology not yet quite forgotten.

In all this, however, we can barely detect a trace of the dialectic which characterizes the Barthian School so essentially that it justifies their favorite title, Dialectical Theology. For there is no dialectic in the denial of sheer falsehood. And, above, it was to the falsehoods of our common creed I drew attention, without lingering to consider how much of truth there may be in it. Dialectic emerges in the tension between truth and truth—between two truths which are really or apparently opposite, or at least not obviously concordant. Dialectic, therefore, expresses itself in paradox—of necessity, and not as a whim. I cannot lead you further till you get some idea of what the Dialectical School means by dialectic. For though this word denotes a method, it must be understood as a method essential to the School of Crisis—which would cease to be what it is, if it should cease to be dialectical. This suggests a danger which is not imaginary. For the dialectical method is not one which everybody can handle or likes to handle. It is a gift, a disposition. Barth would not have learned it from Kierkegaard, the great master of dialectic, unless he himself had had a preëminent disposition for it. Even now, in the character of a dogmatist, he does not abate the rigorous consistency of this method. He continues to turn a deaf ear to the many appeals that he adopt finally a positive *position*, clearly defined against all other possible positions. He replies that his "position" is like that of a bird in flight. Or by a more pedestrian figure he describes himself as a "viator"—always on the march, or, by an Alpine analogy, as a climber on the knife edge of an arête, shrinking from the abyss on either side, and unable to keep his balance except by going on. This does not mean that he goes on triumphantly, leaving behind him the firm positions which he has acquired. For these "positions" remain just as precarious for one who comes after him. I have used just now Kierkegaard's phrase which scornfully describes Hegel's dialectical method: "He then goes on!" Having established, that is to say, one secure position after another (each one serving in turn as a base for the next hop, skip and a jump), "he then goes on" (with his thesis, antithesis and synthesis) to explain the whole of existence. Barth's early critics lifted up hands of horror at the mere mention of such a word as dialectic—for in Germany Hegel is no longer held in high honor. They ought to have observed, however, this very essential difference, that Barth does not go on . . . to the synthesis. He learned his dialectical method, not from Hegel, but from Kierkegaard —who believed in his turn that he had learned it from Socrates. Even if this opinion of Kierkegaard's may be open to doubt, his method is not thereby invalidated. It is the dialectical method, however, more than any inherent obscurity, that accounts for the impression that Barth's teaching is hard to understand. Many people are not capable of believing that the paradox is all he ventures to offer them, that instead of going on triumphantly to resolve by a synthesis the paradoxical thesis and antithesis, he stops short and contents himself with the wholeness which is divined but is not perceived in a balanced pair of opposite truths. Or rather, because the balance is unstable, he does not "stop," but moves almost instantaneously from the one to the other in the "dialectical moment." There are many who cannot content themselves with that attitude, which is not a stable "position." Not all the members of the Dialectical School are equally dialectical. Brunner, it seems to me, is not so dialectically inclined as Barth. He is disposed to take unequivocal and firm positions, both positively and negatively. Perhaps it is for that reason interpreters of the Barthian theology prefer to quote him rather than Barth or Gogarten, and perhaps it is for that reason I quote him here. It is manifestly difficult to describe a theology which takes no positions. And perhaps that is a reason why Paul Tillich holds aloof. But for that there is also another reason—namely, the fact that Tillich is impatient to go on to *practical* conclusions, to *Gestaltung* and *Verwirklichung* (*i.e.* to a practical re*form*ation of society by putting genuine Christian ideals into effect). His impatience finds a sympathetic echo in our activistic civilization. Some berate Barth because, having begun as a socialist of the school of Ragaz, he now is content to be simply a theologian. Many more will feel that this time in which we live cries loudly for formative effort and the practical realization of ideals. For in this chaotic time our life lacks form, it lacks "style." That is the railing accusation of Oswald Spengler, and it is true. I am not indisposed to admit that we may justly detect here a limitation of Karl Barth. In this respect he is not like Kierkegaard, who died fighting for realizations. And yet it is a limitation I do not resent. Man kann nur etwas nicht alles werden. And in this time of transition a theologian may be counted excusable if he does not presume to know *what* form can and must be impressed upon society—or upon the Church. *Between the Times* (*Zwischen den Zeiten*) is the significant title the Barthian School has chosen for its bimonthly review. Partly this has reference to the time just before us and the better time soon to come. We really are living in a transitional period; and much as it needs form-giving (*Gestaltung*), it is not so obvious *how* this is to be given. But "Between the Times" certainly has also a much larger significance, for it refers to eternity at *both* ends of time, the *arche* and the *telos,* the Beginning and the End. Between them lies *all* time. For time is finite. And one who understands how time is conditioned by the End will not be tempted to build Towers of Babel, but will go about his form-giving and realization of ideals with a chastened spirit. Barth does not presume to restrain us from the pursuit of such activities. Practically, I find in his doctrine incitement to do and to dare (just as Albert Schweitzer's eschatology prompts one to "live dangerously"), although in the same dialectical moment one is convinced that "all is vanity." "Therefore strive!" would be Kierkegaard's conclusion. *That* is dialectic! Schweitzer's phrase, "interim ethics," which originated with Johannes Weiss, has met with general reprobation—I cannot get it through my stupid head *why*. And I have reason to fear that I shall not commend the Barthian theology when I call it *interim theology*. But that is what a theology must be which knows itself to be "between the Times"—that is to say, under the sign of finitude, which admonishes us that it is not possible for man to know or think or say anything direct and positive and unequivocal about God, but only indirectly, reflectedly, refractively (like "a straight staff bent in the pool")—

> Thus making Him broken lights
> And a stifled splendor and gloom.

Precisely what the Dialectical School means by dialectic you can best understand by examples. And the most exemplary examples that occur to me are selections from the Diaries of Kierkegaard which Diem translates into German and publishes in *Zwischen den Zeiten*.[2] From this selection I choose only a few. They are examples of dialectical paradox which will not seem fantastic to you, because they deal with the familiar antithesis between man's work and God's work, Law and Gospel. Here it is more precisely the contrast between the *immitatio Christi* and divine

---

[2] 9 Jahrgang, 1931, Heft 1.

grace. Like us, Kierkegaard puts the practical duties of discipleship *first* and conceives of the "following" of Jesus as *immitatio*. Like us, too, he is inclined to linger exclusively upon *this* term of the paradox—as if there were no paradox. But you are to note that when he puts "grace" *last* he puts it where it receives the strongest accent.

"I must now take good care (or I had better say, God will take good care for me) that I be not bewildered by fixing my gaze one-sidedly upon Christ as Example. That is the dialectical moment to the next, which regards Christ as Gift, as one who (according to Luther's constant distinction) was bestowed upon us. But dialectical as my nature is, in the passion of dialectics it always seems as if the opposite thought simply did not exist—and hence this (the thought of the *immitatio*) is always first and strongest."

"In the recognition of the contemporaneousness of Christ you discover that you never succeed in being like him. Not even in what you call your highest moment. For in such a moment you do not experience the appropriate tension of reality, but reflect upon it with the aloofness of a spectator. Hence it follows that you profitably learn to flee to faith and grace. The Example is that which makes endless demands upon you, and you feel terribly the unlikeness—then you flee *to* the Example, and he will have mercy upon you. Thus the Example is he who most sternly and endlessly condemns you—and at the same time it is he who has mercy upon you."

In this connection it occurs to me to translate one of Rückert's *Strung Pearls*, the first line of which he borrows from the Koran:—

> From God there is no flight but only to him.
> Against a father's sternness no revolt avails,
> The child's sole refuge is within his arms.

"The following of Jesus—though it be prosecuted with the most strenuous effort—should only be like a jest, something childish, if by it we think to accomplish something serious, that is, before God and in the direction of merit—the Atonement is the serious thing. But it is horrible that men, 'because there is such a thing as grace,' will use it as an excuse for making no effort."

This is an appropriate place to interject a saying of Kierkegaard's which is found in his *Philosophical Fragments*:

"To abbreviate the hours of sleep by night, and to buy up every hour of the day, without sparing oneself —and then to understand that all this is jest . . . that is earnestness indeed!"

"Only in this way can man be supported in effort. In order to gain courage to strive one must rest in the blessed assurance that all is already decided, that he has already conquered—in faith and through faith."

And here finally is a paragraph which is especially instructive to us and is much more than a formal paradigm of dialectical method.

"Only with respect to that which is on the same level with ourselves can there be any question of merit —as with respect to the fulfillment of a 'claim' upon us. But 'grace' has placed itself endlessly high above you, and therefore it makes meritoriousness impossible. Hence 'grace' is on the one hand the expression of God's endless love, but at the same time and in the highest degree it is an expression of majesty which indicates God's infinite sublimity. In view of the distance of 'grace' you are endlessly further from God than you are put by the distance of the Law and its claim upon you (though in another respect you are endlessly nearer—that is, when you take refuge in his love which is hidden under 'grace'). For with respect to the Law and its claims upon you, it is as if God stooped to contend with you; and on the other hand you might imagine it possible for you to achieve the fulfillment of the Law. But with respect to the distance of 'grace' God has placed you once for all at an endless distance—in order that he might have mercy upon you. At the same time that God in Christ came infinitely nearer to men, in 'grace,' he assured for himself therewith an infinitely more majestic expression for the *distance*—that is, for the name of 'grace.' "

I am well aware that I have not expounded the Barthian theology seductively. I cannot present it truly and clearly except as "foolishness" and as a "stumbling-block." That is what the Gospel is today, as much as it was at the beginning—except as we have deformed it to suit the present taste. I have sought importunately to press it upon you as *your* crisis,—to wrench you out of the superior and secure position of a spectator. Accordingly I have not represented Barth's protest as directed against the theology of Schleiermacher, Ritschl, Otto and other Germans, but as applying precisely and directly to the principal tenets of our modernistic theology. To be sure, it would be well for you to realize that our modern Liberalism was "made in Germany," and that we have contributed to it not one original thought. For then you might look expectantly to Germany for the cure of it. There where the virus has worked longest and most virulently you might hope to find the defensive antitoxin. For the situation of Christianity in Germany is evidently more perilous than here. And for that reason may perhaps be accounted more hopeful —as when a sickness has reached its crisis. (This is one of the implications of the title "School of Crisis.") For until man has reached the end of his tether, and in his extremity is compelled to hear the divine *Stop!* God has no opportunity. In a book published only in French Unamuno envisages even "the death pangs of Christianity" (*L'agonie du Christianisme*) as God's opportunity. But he has been taught by Kierkegaard to think chiefly in terms of the individual. *Agonia* is his rendering of Kierkegaard's "Anguish."[a] And he has small hopes of a man until he has come, not with a "cold doubt" but in fear and trembling, *desesperado,* to the brink of the abyss. Kierkegaard describes paradoxically even that moment when a man heeds God's voice as a "comforted despair." Heidegger, for the purposes of metaphysical argument, as I have said, generalizes Kierkegaard's notion of anguish and speaks only of *Sorge*—anxious care. But in the end he is more terrible than his master when he writes (with italics and with heavy-faced type) of the moment of *decision* in which man is delivered from his *perdition in the world* and becomes himself, by the passionate, illusionless, factual, self-conscious and anguished *openness to death* (*Freiheit zum Tode*) as his utmost and most intrinsic human possibility.[b]

I return now nearer to the surface when I remark that you cannot be expected to embrace with enthusiasm a dialectical method, which is confessedly "broken" thinking (argument in broken lines) so long as you are confident that it is perfectly possible for man in time to speak adequately and directly about eternity and about God, and so long as boundless credulity ascribes to Science the power to explain all

---

[a] *Der Begriff der Angst* is the title of one of Kierkegaard's most powerful works.
[b] *Sein und Zeit,* p. 266 *et passim.* Here I have rendered freely a passage which as a whole could not be understood out of its context.

the problems of existence, even the deepest—or at the least to prove that there is nothing very deep. In Germany not only, but everywhere on the Continent of Europe men have ceased to hold science in extravagant reverence. They are even questioning whether the very foundations of the natural sciences are securely laid. The Darwinian theory of biological evolution is universally discarded. And where an evolutionary philosophy exists, optimism has been eliminated from it. In all these respects their situation is more hopeful than ours. In Germany especially, we can easily perceive how great an advantage it is to such men as Barth that they have no pragmatic philosophy to contend with, and no behaviorist psychology. With the "deep psychology" of Freud and Jung and Adler they can come to terms, and still more easily with the deeper introspective psychology sponsored by the Phenomenological School. Though Barth is chary of accepting any philosophy as an ally of theology (considering that the philosophers have and must have a very different aim), he reaps no small advantage from the fact that Heidegger speaks the language of Kierkegaard.

In none of these respects are we so fortunate. I have said that the situation of Christianity in Germany is evidently more perilous than here. Perhaps it would be more true to say that it is more evidently perilous. That, it seems, is what Barth thinks. For though he recognizes (with a comforted despair) that Christianity everywhere shows signs of dissolution, he remarks that only in America are we intent upon seeing to it that it dies *beautifully*—"preparing for it a euthanasia." Not long ago, when on Thanksgiving Day I was escorting a Methodist minister to my pulpit, I was moved to say to him brusquely, "*You are no better than we are.*" "True," he replied, "we too are building million dollar churches." But building churches on the installment plan is not the only way we show our zeal to prepare for Christianity its euthanasia.

In America our plight is not *essentially* different from the plight of the Protestant churches in Germany—only we do not perceive it so clearly. We can boast of more evident signs of ecclesiastical stability; but it would be wise for us to recognize that what we most boast of, whether they be ritual embellishments or triumphs of social service, might be described in Ruskin's phrase as "parasitical sublimities," in comparison with the essential notes of Christianity. Even here our ebullient optimism and our blind belief in the inevitability of progress has lately been checked by a shock which seems trivial to the European. When we are financially "broke" we are in a position to understand what Barth means by "brokenness." He does not use this word *only* of the broken line of dialectical thought, to indicate that *straight* thinking about God and eternity is not a human possibility, and indeed that we can know nothing about God except as he has revealed himself. He uses it more commonly to denote our moral bankruptcy—not the bare fact of it, but a conscious recognition of it. It means the brokenness of spirit which the Psalmist had in mind. The flesh is always under condemnation: "They who are in the flesh cannot please God." The question is whether we recognize how fragile we are, and how problematical, how questionable is everything that we can boast of—even when we have become Christians "according to the flesh." For in fact it is the Christians especially, if not exclusively, who in this sense are "broken" and know it. Mindful of a phrase already quoted from Kierkegaard, we might call this brokenness of ours a comforted brokenness. At all events, we must reflect that, if Christians should claim to be unbroken, then in this whole world there are no "broken spirits"—no men at all whom God will not despise.

In this lecture I have briefly referred to almost all the themes which are distinctive to the Barthian theology. In the following lectures we shall have time to consider more fully only a few of the principal topics. I have made it clear that Barth's protest is chiefly against Liberal Theology, in its positive as well as in its negative aspects. Against its positive aspects most of all. For you hardly need to be told that it is not aimed against the results of Biblical criticism—however negative they may seem to be. An obscurantist theology could gain no ascendancy in Germany. It is aimed, as you doubtless have heard with surprise, also against orthodoxy. And you may be puzzled to know what that can mean, when you are told in the same breath that Barthianism is a return to the theology of the Reformation. Evidently it is not simply a return, a reactionary return, to the Protestant orthodoxy of the seventeenth century. It could not be that, because it is dialectical. What it protests against in Protestant orthodoxy and in every other orthodoxy is the assumption that man can say anything directly, positively and unparadoxically about God, can occupy assured positions—"and then go on." But that is also its complaint against Liberal Theology in its most positive aspects. Nothing is more *unbroken* than the confidence of the Liberal that he possesses the truth. Liberalism is only apparently a system of doubt. It deals, in fact, coldly with many doubts; but it does not suffer to emerge the one hot and devastating doubt which impugns our faith in . . . Man. So the Barthian School wages war on the right hand and on the left. Yet there is a very great difference in the pathos of these two protests. It coldly declines to ally itself with orthodoxy—but hotly it attacks the positive Liberalism, in which it discovers a zeal to exalt man . . . at the expense of God. But evidently it is against pietism also, the sole warm remnant of Evangelicalism, which exalts its questionable experiences and problematical goodness into a proof of the existence of God.

It is not surprising that the Barthian theology is not welcomed in the United States. The Fundamentalists cannot thole it because it refuses to attach any great religious importance to Biblical criticism. And what else have we here but Liberalism and Catholicism? For Liberalism is not confined to the large and self-confident school which cuts athwart all denominational lines, but it has deeply impregnated the old Evangelical parties in all the Churches, and Anglo-Catholicism is by no means free from its influence. It still predominates in the pew *and* in the pulpit. *But* I perceive now, on my return from a residence of many years in Europe, that it no longer sits in the highest places. Not in such places, I mean, as Union Seminary, or the Harvard Theological School, or our own Divinity School in Cambridge. For the watchmen in those high places have seen what has happened in the homeland of Liberal Theology, where the most outstanding Liberal leaders (Prof. Troeltsch at the head of them) have conceded that Liberalism, though it is the only form in which Christianity can be held today by enlightened men, is *not* Christianity. That concession puts an end to a vast deal of hypocrisy; and it ushers in a new era, in which Radicalism must increase at the expense of Liberalism, because it has stolen the glamour from it. The Liberals may be just as liberal as ever, but in the eyes of the Radicals they are conservatives. To religious Liberalism the same thing has happened that has overwhelmed political Liberalism. It is no longer at the head of the column. It has been forced back to a middle position where it cannot but be suspected of compromise.

LECTURE II

THE TELOS

THE PROBLEM OF TIME

Contemplating such a phenomenon as the School of Crisis, one is compelled to assume that there is some *principle* which holds it together, and which makes it *one* in spite of the dissimilarity of the minds which compose it. For even if we speak of it as the Barthian School, we must be aware that it is not held together simply by personal allegiance to the one master. These are "disciples" who do not scruple to criticise their master. Gogarten in particular questions the positive development of Barth's thought in his *Dogmatik,* and he assumes to do so on the basis of the principle which informs the Dialectical Theology. When we embrace in our view other scholars who disclaim to be followers of Barth, though they acknowledge an initial indebtedness to him, it is still more evident that there must be a common principle which accounts for their agreement upon the fundamental topics which I propose to dwell upon here. In spite of Barth's reluctance to systematize theology, we have reason to suspect that there must be some criterion which, if we could discover it, would enable us to detect theology of crisis under whatever name we may find it, to determine, with regard to any proposition which is presented to us, whether it is consonant with this theology or no. In fact Barth has stated this principle with the utmost emphasis in a place which stands under the strongest accent.

In the preface to the second edition of his *Romans,* replying to the charge that he has interpreted St. Paul to suit his "system," he remarks, "If I have any 'system,' it consists in this, that I keep as steadily as possible in view what Kierkegaard has called 'the infinite qualitative difference' between time and eternity, and that both in its positive and in its negative aspects. 'God is in heaven and thou upon earth.'"

This principle Barth has stated in many other places, and it is often repeated by his followers. Naturally, none of his interpreters has failed to observe its importance. I am bold enough to assume that in stating this principle Barth has furnished us with a clue which enables every man to construct his own Barthian theology. If I had but one hour in which to expound the Barthian Theology, I believe I could do it most effectively and expeditiously by simply deducing it from this proposition. I use here the word "deduce" because I want to say emphatically that it is *not* the right word. *Nothing* can be deduced from the infinite qualitative difference between time and eternity—unless it be man's absolute incapacity to know God. Speaking properly, I would say that we can construct the Theology of Crisis by keeping "as steadily as possible in view" this critical principle. For this critical principle not only justifies the dialectical method of "broken" thought, as the only appropriate and possible way of thinking about God and eternity; but evidently it cuts trenchantly athwart all the characteristic pronouncements of our modern theology, which, as an evolutionary theology of progress, is founded upon belief in continuity as between time and eternity, and as between man and God, allowing only a quantitative difference. Barth is never tired of asserting that from man to God there is no way, nor from time to eternity—but only from God to man, and from eternity to time.

If so much (indeed everything) is made to depend upon this principle, it must be proved before we go any further. Rather its validity must be recognized. For how can so fundamental a principle be proved?

In conferences and animated debate about the Barthian Theology I have been surprised to find that there is very little disposition to dispute the proposition that there is an infinite qualitative difference between time and eternity. Yet until now we have all been operating unquestioningly with the notion that eternity is nothing more than the infinite prolongation of time—that it is essentially *time,* conceived of as infinitely prolonged in both directions. When a man like Ernest Häckel scornfully referred to this conception as "a spurious eternity," it may be supposed that he was not so much questioning our idea of infinite time as discarding the notion that there is such a thing as eternity. Plato operated with the idea of infinite time. Wherefore he had no place for eternity but along side of time, or rather above it, in the realm of "ideas," which touched time at no point, and therefore, in spite of the infinite qualitative difference, had no conflict with it. Hence time was not a problem for Plato. Nor has it been felt as a problem by any of the philosophers until our day. When Bergson[1] drew our attention emphatically to the puzzles involved in our notion of time (which he thought of as

---

[1] In *Evolution creatrice,* but more particularly in his *Essai sur les données immédiates de la conscience,* translated by Pogson with the title *Time and Free Will.*

"pure duration") and to its relation to space,[a] he was not thinking of its relation to eternity, and was therefore unaware of the *serious* problem. Nevertheless, his book was prophetic because it brought Time into the lime-light, though in fact he did little more than revert to the old puzzle of Zeno's about Achilles and the tortoise.

In the meantime we have gone on just as before with a notion of infinite time which involved no paradox. The immortality of the soul we have thought of sometimes as an endless prolongation of life in time—and when that became too difficult we have been accustomed to switch over to Plato's eternity, without noticing in the least how radical was the change of categories. We understood Plato's eternity to be equivalent to the Christian notion of heaven. For Plato's notion of the immortality of the soul in an eternity *above* infinite time was long ago thoroughly assimilated by the Church. It naturally appealed to early Catholicism as the most congenial element discoverable in pagan thought. It was not far to seek, for it had already been popularized in the mystery cults. For a long while it occupied a place side by side with the characteristic Christian hope, the resurrection of the dead—which really was a totally different thought, because it was eschatological, referring not to a *there* but to a *then,* not to a heaven above but to the "kingdom" which is to come. In our day the Platonic immortality has almost entirely usurped the place of the Christian thought. We have been under the impression that it is an *easier* thought

---

[a] "It is principally by the help of motion that duration assumes the form of a homogeneous medium and that time is projected into space." P. 124 of the translation. And "time, conceived under the form of an unbounded and homogeneous medium, is nothing more than the ghost of space haunting the reflective consciousness." P. 99,

to entertain, and we have not reflected that Plato could no more admit than does Barth that there is any real passage from time to eternity. The soul that ceases to exist in time does not *pass* into eternity, but may take what comfort it can from the thought that its "idea" still is conserved timelessly in eternity. Or if a livelier hope could be entertained, unsupported by philosophy, it was only as a *kalon kindunon*, a beautiful risk—which is something different from "the sure and certain hope of everlasting life." Because it contemplated no tension between time and eternity, neither Platonism nor Neoplatonism was a force which operated to change the actual world. It encouraged quietism, not reformation. Plato's fine words at the end of *The Republic*[8] have only a superficial resemblance to the words of Jesus about the kingdom of God—to whom the assurance that there "*will be* such a city" was anything but a matter of indifference! Without perceiving the problem of time which is inherent in eschatology, if it is taken seriously, theologians as well as philosophers have skimmed triumphantly over it. And they have skimmed over Biblical eschatology as well, regarding it as a thing too hard to believe; whereas, if they had learned even to state correctly the problem of time, they might have seen that it was an inevitable belief.

If there had not occurred within the last few years a radical change in the intellectual climate, it seems to me likely that Barth would have been, like Kirkegaard, a voice crying in the wilderness. I do not know whether the first hint of change, and the first

---

[8] "In heaven there is laid up a pattern of such a city, and he who desires may behold this, and beholding, govern himself accordingly. But whether there really is or ever will be such an one is of no importance to him; for he will act according to the laws of that city and of no other." Jowett's translation.

impulse towards it, was or was not Einstein's theory of the relativity of time, and the idea of "space-time" which Minkowski contributed. Certainly we experienced a severe shock in the mere suggestion that time might be finite. And in the last few years the problem of time has become the chief problem of philosophy.

Now we are able to take seriously St. Augustine's agitated discussion of time in the eleventh book of his *Confessions,* whereas a while ago even theologians wondered why the saint should have invented so many difficulties to worry about. Now the most modern philosophers are quoting freely from this book; and if you will permit me to recite here some passages at random, they may not sound antiquated to you.

§ 14. "For what is time? Who can easily and briefly explain what it is? Who even can comprehend it in thought so as to be able to speak about it? Yet what is there we talk about more familiarly than time, as if we knew quite well what it is? And in fact we do understand what we mean when we speak of time, and when another speaks about it we understand him. As long as no one asks me, I know; but if I try to explain it to an inquirer, I do not know. Nevertheless I am presumptuous enough to think that I know *this*: that if nothing passed away, time past were not; and if nothing were coming to pass, a future time were not; and if nothing existed now, present time were not. (In § 30 he says, "Let them see therefore that time cannot be without created being.") How then do these two times, past and future, *exist,* seeing that what is past no longer exists, and what is still to come does not yet exist? And the present, if it should always remain present and never vanish into the past, would not indeed be time but eternity. To become time, then, the present must become past

—and how can we say that even this exists when the ground of its existence is that it ceases to exist? It seems as if we could not say that time *is* except as it ceases to be. § 15. Let us see then, thou soul of man, whether present time can be long; for to thee it is given to feel and to measure the length of time. § 27. It is in thee, my mind, I measure times. § 23. I perceive time to be a sort of extension. But do I perceive this or only seem to perceive it? § 26. Does not my soul most truly confess unto Thee that I do measure time? Do I then measure, O my God, without knowing what I measure? I measure the motion of a body in time, but time itself I do not measure. . . . Whence it seems to me that time is nothing else but extension—but extension of what I know not, and I wonder if it may not be of the mind itself."

My reason for consuming so much of your *time* with this long quotation from St. Augustine is that I would call your attention to the significant fact that he was dealing with the problem of time, not as a philosopher (for this problem had escaped the attention of all the philosophers), but as a theologian, and that he was obliged to deal with it in this place because he was engaged here in explaining the first chapter of Genesis, which, taken seriously, contemplates a real beginning, the Beginning, and implies therefore an end, the End. That is to say, it was the thought of the *Arche* and the *Telos* (and of Christ as the Alpha and Omega, the Beginning and the End —which is the essence of Christian eschatology) that obliged St. Augustine to struggle with the problem of time. Whereas today the situation is exactly reversed: it is the problem of time, rightly stated at last, which compels us again to take seriously the *Arche* and *Telos*—that is, to adopt the eschatological orientation, not looking any longer up and down, or around about, but backwards and forwards. This is indubitably the orientation which Jesus sought to impress upon his disciples.

Karl Heim, the philosophical theologian of Tübingen, observes that in this century we have not only attained a "different conception of time" but have a "different time-feeling." It is not clear which came first. But at all events it is significant that this new feeling has found expression only within the last decade, and chiefly within the past four years. Prof. Alexander[4] admonishes us to "take time seriously." We have been taking it too seriously, I should think. Till a short while ago, under the impression of the old time-feeling, we lightly assumed that it was perfectly easy to think of time as endless and quite impossible to think of it as finite—although in fact the well known antinomy of Kant offered us only the choice of two impossible possibilities. Now we perceive that in this hard dilemma Kant did not rightly state the problem of time, and pretty generally it is agreed that we *must* think of time as finite. This is conceded by H. B. Schmidt.[5] Though his book entitled *Time and Eternity* is directed against the Dialectical School, yet it assumes also the qualitative difference between time and eternity. Karl Heim[6] expresses the new idea of time with greater incisiveness. Because the English translation of his work is available I need not quote from it. Though he is regarded as the

---
[4] *Time, Space and Deity,* Bampton Lectures, 1918.
[5] *Zeit und Ewigkeit,* 1928.
[6] The chapter on *Time and Eternity,* in a work of his translated by Dickie and published by the Christian Student Movement, 1930. Also in *Glaube und Denken,* 1931, pp. 139-164, 381-388. I would mention also Husserl, *Vorlesungen zur Phänomenologie des inneren Zeitbewustseins,* 1928; and Eberhard Griesbach, *Gegenwart, eine kritische Ethik,* 1928. As I am not a philosopher, it is probable that I am not acquainted with all the recent pronouncements upon this theme.

rival of Barth, he is on this point in substantial agreement with him. Unfortunately Martin Heidegger's amazing ontology entitled *Being and Time*[1] is written in a language which is untranslatable, though in German it is in the highest degree picturesque. According to Heidegger, time is the meaning of all existence, the meaning of the substance of all temporal being. This may seem to be a way of taking time too seriously. But it is assumed here that time is finite, and therefore it is implied that existence as we know it (temporal being) comes to an end along with time. Beyond that is eternity, characterized by an infinite qualitative difference. "The things that are seen are temporal, the things that are not seen are eternal."

I mention Heidegger last because his philosophy points so emphatically to the End—and it is the End, the Telos, we are now about to consider.

---

[1] *Sein und Zeit*, 1926.

THE TELOS

I am confident that I have not been wandering from my theme in a disquisition which may seem to you too philosophical. It is a way (and I think the only secure way) of introducing you, not only to, but deeply into the Theology of Crisis—particularly into that part of it which is most difficult for you, the Barthian eschatology. For we must confess to ourselves that hitherto the eschatology of the Gospel has seemed not only difficult to us but impossible. No one today can escape the challenging fact that the Gospel of Jesus was *essentially* eschatological. No one has put this so clearly—so ruthlessly, we may feel—as Albert Schweitzer. And yet he himself, for lack of an appropriate time-feeling or time-idea, could not become a believing eschatologist. We cannot expect to make our own the eschatological expectation of the New Testament without severe and prolonged mental labor.

Barth, it may seem, arrived without effort. There can be no rounder affirmation than his: "A Christianity which is not altogether and utterly eschatological has altogether and utterly nothing to do with Jesus Christ." Yet his interpreters, beginning with Strauch,[*] express a doubt whether he is a thoroughgoing eschatologist—or whether, at least, he did not have to overcome gradually a certain reluctance before he accepted the eschatological outlook of the New Testament. This, I am sure, is a misunder-

[*] *Die Theologie Karl Barths.*

standing of the situation. For, so far as we are permitted to see, it seems rather as if Barth became with one spring a thoroughgoing eschatologist. He leapt at once into the heart of eschatology when he embraced Kierkegaard's dictum that there is an infinite qualitative difference between time and eternity. When that dictum is accepted with the understanding that time is finite, it means that time issues from eternity as its "Source" and returns to it as its "Goal." I emphasize Source and Goal because they are the words Barth prefers. "Source" is a word he was familiar with in Neo-Kantian philosophy, where it has implications which are not all of them appropriate in this connection. More familiar and more expressive are the Scriptural words *Arche* and *Telos*—Beginning and End. Inasmuch as *end* is a word which may mean to us merely an extremity or termination, and does not necessarily carry the implication of consummation, fulfillment—an end to which toil and purpose are coöperant—I prefer to use here the Greek word *Telos* to denote "the last things." Now the point I wish to make is that Barth did not approach this question, as most of us have done, from the outside, haggling about this or that Biblical expression; but from the inside, that is, from the point of view from which the eschatological outlook was a necessity and it was possible to question only the pictorial forms in which it expressed itself. There is no room for serious quarrel about these forms, for in the nature of the case they can only be more or less appropriate, never absolutely adequate. We must not be led astray by the fact that Barth characterizes as "a myth" the forms which are used in the Bible to express the eschatological hope. This does not mean that he repudiates them. For today the word myth is not used in Germany simply as a synonym for unreality. I myself, as a believing eschatologist, use the word myth to characterize the Biblical picture of the "last things" because it is the most significant word I can use. It is significant *because* it associates the Biblical account of the End with the mythical account of the Beginning. In neither respect does the word myth disparage the Biblical account—except in so far as it implies that *any* intelligible account of what lies beyond time, at either end, must in the nature of the case be inadequate and merely figurative. For if we take seriously the qualitative difference between time and eternity, we have to recognize that it is impossible for man in time to form any valid positive conception of eternity, even though it be but a hair's breadth before time or after it. And not only of what lies beyond time, but even of what lies just this side of eternity, at the two points where time issues from its Source and disappears in its Goal. For those two "times" are so profoundly qualified by eternity that they cannot be regarded as homogeneous with the time which history takes account of. If we are not satisfied with describing both these times negatively— "what eye hath not seen, neither ear heard, neither hath it entered into the heart of man to believe"—we

---

[9] Partly as a consequence of a revival of the theory of J. J. Bachofen (or perhaps as a cause of it?), a new edition of his work was published in 1926, with the title *Der Mythus von Orient und Occident*. Cp. Erich Unger, *Das Problem der mythischen Realität*, David Verlag, Berlin, 1926. Philologists who follow this lead claim to find in mythology a clue to realities of pre-history, which history properly so called was too late to catch a glimpse of. And a German scientist, Edgar Dacqué, finds in the Biblical myths information regarding the formation of this terrestrial globe. The three books he has written are highly interesting, even if they be not convincing. *Urwelt, Sage und Menschheit*, 1924; *Natur und Seele*, 1926; *Leben als Symbol*, 1927. Somewhat in the same character is a strange (but by no means negligible) book by a conservative Jewish scholar, Oscar Goldberg: *Die Wirklichkeit der Hebräer*, 1925.

must at least recognize that we are dealing with myth. Here myth is to be understood as an effort to conceive of eternity by pictures drawn from the time-form, which is the only illustrative material available to us. Barth rightly protests against the notion that the End and the signs which accompany or precede it belong to history. That *seems* to be the implication of the Biblical account; but we are convinced that it is not its *meaning*, in the deepest sense. For though, in the nature of the case, this seems to be the implication of *every* mythical account, yet evidently it is *not* its meaning.

It may be that the only large bodies of Christians that still exemplify the orientation which Jesus emphatically impressed upon his disciples—the attitude of joyful expectation and watchful waiting—are the ignorant and enthusiastic sects which look for the kingdom of God to come (that is for Christ to come) *within* history and before the abolition of the time form. We cannot share such expectations, and we are ill at ease because we imagine that we therefore cannot share the expectation which Jesus had and which he inspired in his disciples. And we are conscious that we have not been able to construe Christianity coherently without it. But that hope in its essence we can share—watching, waiting, expecting, living as on the brink. And Barth, more than any other man of our time helps us to do so. That is his supreme value to me. And I have taken so much pains to lead you to this point in order that you may hear with sympathy as well as with understanding what he has to say about this temporal life as qualified by the End. We *need* to be prepared for this, for it must be confessed that for a long time such thoughts have been strange to us. They came as a shock to all who read them in the *Romans*. It was a shock to hear time disparaged by contrast with eternity. But that was too plain an implication to be resented. And besides it had a brighter side—in the thought that life even now was qualified by the eternity which is to come. Qualified "existentially," but not perceptibly! Far darker, and only too perceptible, is the qualification which life—and all existence—receives from the End as an end.

Death, as the end of the individual life, qualifies the *whole* life, characterizes its every moment as mortal, from infancy to decrepit age. From our intimate experience of the vanity of human life we generalize, and declare that "all is vanity." This judgment embraces all created things, all existence in time. We argue thus naively, hardly conscious of what we do. But we find Heidegger following substantially the same argument as a philosopher and developing it with scrupulous pains. Human life is essentially qualified by the fact that it is a "rushing forward unto death." And as man is the prerogative instance for the philosopher's investigation, inasmuch as he is the only example of existence in time which we can study profoundly, by introspection, it is permissible to generalize from this instance to all temporal existence. Even the anguish which man feels in the experience of his mortality indicates the secret anguish of the universe. This is what St. Paul felt with a universal sympathy sustained by a flaming imagination: "All the creation groans and travails in pain," like ourselves oppressed by the bondage of corruption—and like ourselves it *waits* for the revelation of the glory of the sons of God. The change he expected was complete, involving the whole *schema* of the universe (1 Cor. 7:31).

Death is the one experience in time which is an adequate illustration (or you may prefer to call it parable) of the end of time. You need not be surprised, therefore, that Barth, as an eschatologist, and all his school and all whom I count akin to it, make much of death, and do not even wish to obscure its reality. If it were not the sternest reality, but only (as we are prone to think of it) a transition of merely apparent significance in the continuum of time, it would not be a parable of the End, the true *Telos*. Neither will you be surprised that he makes much of the Resurrection. And you will understand now perhaps why he says that the Resurrection—whether it be the Resurrection at the Last Day or the Resurrection of Jesus —does not belong to history. It cannot belong to history if it is not in time but beyond it—even if only by a hair's breadth.

The theme of death and resurrection is prominent not only in the first book of Barth's, the *Romans*, but in everything he has written. And it is significant that he has singled out for comment the fifteenth chapter of I Corinthians, conceiving of it as the meaning of the whole epistle.[16]

Having brought you to this point so painstakingly, and put you to so much pains to follow me, I will now test your proficiency in the Barthian Theology by reading to you a long passage from the strange commentary I have just mentioned. This will also be a test of my success in expounding this theology. This passage will tell you much if not all that still needs to be said on the subject of this lecture. You will wish to hear Barth speak to you directly, and now I believe you are in a position to understand him. This, remember, is the chapter which we read at the burial of the dead, which therefore is heard, if not more frequently than any other, at least under circumstances

---

[16] *Die Auferstehung der Toten* (The Resurrection of the Dead), 1924.

more solemn. You may not be disposed to expect that there are any thoughts properly associated with the theme of this chapter which you have not already reflected upon. I read you only a small part of the introduction to the comment on the fifteenth chapter, selecting it as a sample, not because it is the best passage I could find, or because I consider it a purple passage, but because in this connection it is the most obvious choice.

"It cannot be by mere chance that 1 Cor. 15, a chapter which is one of the most positive that can be conceived of, constitutes the climax and crown of this essentially critical and polemically negative epistle. It is the key passage of the Pauline writings which here is disclosed to us. *Anastasis nekron* (resurrection of the dead) denominates the spot from which Paul speaks and to which he points. From that point of view it is (you are to note) not only the *death* of men now living which is contemplated in the Apostolic sermon, but it is their whole life *on this side* of the threshold of death which is contemplated, understood, estimated, when it is dragged into the light of the austere last moment—and of the final hope. Our reflections have already showed us what Paul understood by this. It means placing the life of men (contemplated in its heights and in its depths) in the light of the great Answer, which precisely at the threshold of death replies to all man's questions. The great Answer which, however, for the fact that it is given precisely *there,* first prompts all the questions of life and combines them in a single great question: which can encounter man only as the question of all questions, and only in this disguise as a question can be understood as an answer. The fifteenth chapter contains doctrine about 'the last things.' This expression inevitably suggests the notion of events and figures which lie in a dim future, whether it be immediately 'at the door,' or perhaps thousands and many thousands of years away, as the far off future, temporally conceived, of the world, of mankind and of the individual—the 'final history,' in the sense of the conclusion of history, history at the conclusion of history, the conclusion of the life history of the individual as well as of world history and Church history, and even of natural history, lying beyond all the possibilities we are acquainted with, yet as new possibilities on a line with the well known possibilities and in continuous sequence with them, although perhaps it will be under the pressure of unheard of catastrophies that these possibilities survive and persist upon a higher plane. Why should there not be such 'final history'—'last things' also in this sense? Why are they not worthy of earnest consideration? The efforts which have been made in all centuries and in all civilizations (which cannot be successfully repressed, and also have never been conducted entirely without a certain success)—the efforts, I mean to say, to penetrate into the secret of a future existence in time, forbid us, if we are of a reflective disposition, *not* to be willing to reckon in any way, manner or fashion with this cheerful or (if one prefers so to regard it) this uncheerful possibility. It might well be—why not? Beside the great historical upheavals through which civilization has passed, and in one of which we now find ourselves, the almost irrepressible presumption that our so-called modern culture may, in the nearer or further future, be about to precipitate into something even worse of the same sort, may very well incline us to entertain the possibility of a 'final history,' even if provisionally it amounts to no more than a new glacial age, such as plays so great a rôle in Troeltsch's theology—that some such catastrophe, I say, might sweep (and certainly not undeservedly!) over the whole world. And when the extinction of a star in the vast dome of night accidentally makes us aware that somewhere, in an entirely unbelievable and unintelligible distance of decades or centuries, a world has perhaps actually and literally perished and been dissolved into its atoms, the remark that such a thing occurred far from here and a long while ago, is at least less clever than the other which is more obvious to a simple mind, namely, *Jam proximus ardet Ucalegon,* just such a thing might occur to us today. As a *parable* of the 'last things' such a far and yet near-lying possibility might indeed be thoroughly instructive and stimulating—especially in view of the fact that we are unfortunately too dull to recognize as parables of the 'last things' the nearer events which press upon our attention in history and at the present moment—without needing to appeal to metempsychosis, glacial periods, and the destiny of extinguished stars. But 'last things' in the sense of 1 Cor. 15, and in the sense of the New Testament as a whole, *such* final possibilities are *not,* however real they may seem in our eyes. Not even then when we conceive of them as preliminary only to psychical-metaphysical-cosmical-metacosmical changes and revolutions of an unimaginable sort. And not even then when the picture of these theosophical 'end-histories' is composed and built up of material taken exclusively from the Bible and perhaps especially from 1 Cor. 15. All that is transitory is *merely* a parable. That also the objects of the Biblical world of imagery belong to the transitory, that they are there to serve and not to dominate, to signify something rather than to *be* anything—about that the Bible itself at least leaves us in no doubt. Last *things* are as such not *last* things, however great and significant they may be. About *last* things we do not speak unless we would speak of the *end* of all things, of their end so absolutely, so fundamentally understood, of a reality so radically superior to all things, that in it the existence of all things is entirely founded, in that alone founded—that is, we would be speaking of an end which would be in truth nothing else but their beginning. Only he truly speaks of end-history and last times who would speak of the *end* of history and of the end of time. But, again, of their end so fundamentally, so absolutely understood, of a reality so radically superior to all occurrences and all that exists in the form of time, that in the fact that he speaks of the finiteness of history and of the finiteness of time, he would be understood in the same breath to speak of that which is at the *foundation* of all time and of all that occurs in time. End-history must for him be equivalent to *pre*-history; the limit of time of which he speaks must be the limit of all and every time, and therefore necessarily the *Source* of time.—Those representations of the 'last things' or of 'end-history' which employ the language of the Bible and its world of ideas (however primitive in certain circumstances they may be) have the great advantage over others of the same sort, that to them the thought of eternity, at least so far as name and place are concerned, is not entirely unknown. The 'last things,' with whatever solemn importance the details may be rehearsed; the final history, however complicatedly it may be spun out, comes here, designedly or undesignedly, to the end of all things, to end-history—in so far as (if the thought of eternity is not altogether unknown) it finally is accustomed to arrive at a particular spot which is the real end, the confluence of all this and that, all here and there, all then and now, in the solemn peace of the One. Here, in case this thought is recognized in its directive power even only in a slight measure, one is at least preserved from casting himself like a drunken man into the bottomless abyss of a supposedly absolute future, as a Wandering Jew through a succession of millions of years, or even a series of aeons, if not exactly to wander, yet to think himself through them, and to conceive that what he brings back from this quest is eschatology. To a mind which is in any way determined by the Bible, the endless series comes somehow and somewhere to a standstill, the endless series therewith becomes finite, in view of the unsurmountable wall which, as God is all in all, is posited by eternity. It cannot here be altogether forgotten and overlooked that eternity (about which perhaps the others speak) is the eternity *of God,* that is to say then, his *reign,* the *kingdom* of God, his preëminent superiority as Creator, Redeemer and King of things and of history—that therefore it emphatically does not mean the endlessness of the world, of time, of things, and of men above all; but, however it may stand with the question of the prolongation of their existence in the beyond, it means radically their finiteness. Such a man as Kuno Fiedler, for example, is consumed by the power of this Biblical notion of eternity as he preaches his passionate gospel of the 'Coming of Nihilism.' But here one must not stop half way. The knowledge that it is the eternity of God which sets a limit to the endlessness of the world, of time, things and of men must be made fruitful. The *last* word that is here spoken must so thoroughly be understood as the last word that it will be understood at the same time as the *first* word, and the history of the end at the same time and as such, as the history of the beginning. As first word and as history of the beginning of all time, of the whole of time, of the earliest as well as of the latest with all the times that lie in between. Time as such is finite by reason of its limitation by eternity. But it [I suppose this means the first-last word] must be understood as the first founding and constituting word and as the history of the beginning, as word and history of the Source of all time, of the whole of time. For when eternity limits time and makes it finite, it posits it indeed as finite, but it *posits* it. When one has made that clear to himself he will be freed from the temptation to confuse the end-history with the final history, however stupendous and wonderful it may be. With respect to the *real* end-history it is appropriate *at every time* to say, The end is near! And even in view of a time of the greatest and most significant catastrophies of a supernatural sort it would not be fundamentally appropriate to say *more* than, The end is near! And that is fundamentally appropriate to yesterday, today, and tomorrow. But he will also be free from another temptation, that of confusing eternity with a great *Nihil*, making out of the end-history a destruction history. That would not be true eternity, the eternity of God, which instead of positing time as finite (*positing* it!), would dissolve it in endlessness. A thinker who would follow through the suggestions of the Bible not only half way but wholly must pass between these two temptations. Doctrine about the 'last things,' or eschatology, is therefore, in case this idea is not very thoroughly cleared up, a misguiding doctrine, and at all events the name is an inadequate characterization of the thought St. Paul exposes in 1 Cor. 15. If we are right in the assumption upon which we have proceeded hitherto in the course of these lectures, that what the Apostle is saying in the whole epistle proceeds from a single point and to this same single point points back, and that 1 Cor. 15 is to be construed as the attempt to express now this one single point by itself, loosed from the associations by which till now it has been half concealed—then is his teaching about the resurrection of the dead which he here expounds anything but an 'eschatology' in the sense which that word has more or less in the conventional treatises on theology, namely, an attempt, after every other possible subject has been discussed, to find something also to say about death, the beyond and the consummation of the world; but his teaching rather has here to do really with *the* 'end' which is also the beginning, with the last things which are at the same time the first. The chapter deals with *death* and with the *dead,* in violent contrast to the fullness of life's possibilities which were the theme of the chapter just before this. All, absolutely all that up to now had been warmly recommended to the Corinthian Christians, here appears suddenly in the drab light of the fact that they must die. Truly it is not a remembrance alongside of other remembrances which Paul would here incite, but it is *the* remembrance. It is about the *resurrection* of the dead that he would speak. That it is which first gives the remembrance meaning and emphasis. What is death to us, if it is only death? What the end, if it is only the end? What eternity, if it is only eternity? What can it matter to us what we are *not,* know *not,* have *not?* But with the word 'resurrection' the Apostolic sermon puts just here in this empty spot, in contrast to all that for us means Being, in contrast to what we know, to what we might possess, in contrast to all things of all time—what? Not the not-being, the unknown, the not to be possessed; but also not a second being, a thing we are to become acquainted with, a higher possession in the future; but the Source and the Truth of all Being, of all that is known, of all that is possessed by us, the reality of all *res,* all things, eternity in time, the *resurrection* of the dead. But mark! All this precisely in that empty spot, precisely there where it seemed that only the indifferent conception of not-being, the unknown, the unapprehensible, had room, where only the dissolution of all things and appearances seemed to be in place, where only the self-contradictory affirmation of the endlessness of time seemed to remain, where dying seemed to be the last word. The dead! That is us. The resurrected! That is not us. But here is precisely what the resurrection of the dead is about—that *that which we are not* is posited as identical with *that which we are*: The dead as alive, time as eternity, being as truth, things as reality. Not otherwise than in hope is all this given—therefore this identity is not to be logically concluded. And so the life which we dead men now live here is *not* to be confused with this other life, about which we always can say only that we do not yet live it. We are not to confuse the endlessness of time with eternity, the materiality of the things that appear with *this* reality, all being which we know or might know with *this* which is its Source. Not to be abolished is the stern fundamental reality of the step which separates this from that as the impossible from the possible—but in hope it is *given;* in hope, in God, the identity of this with that is already concluded, the resurrection of the dead. That is what looms behind the reminder of the fact that we must die, which here at the end of the epistle finally issues upon the stage, after it had far enough cast its shadow before it. Therefore is the reminder of death so momentous, so urgent, so disturbing, so penetrating, because it actually implies the message of the resurrection behind it, is the reminder of *life,* of our life, which we are not living but which yet is our life. Hence it is that the end of the epistle can be also its beginning, the principle which informs it throughout and gives it movement, because it is not merely a conclusion but an end, *telos,* in the sense in which Paul speaks of the End. . . ."

So far Barth. I stop only because we have no time to go further—though I have translated hardly more than one-half of a paragraph which is perhaps the longest that such of you as do not read German have ever stumbled upon. Though I have divided the paragraph, I have taken pains not to divide even the longest sentences, in order that you may have the genuine Barth. You will perhaps conclude that in my exposition I have greatly simplified the Barthian Theology. And perhaps you may not mean that judgment to be disparaging to me. To make things simpler and clearer by means of analysis and coordination is properly the task of an expositor. When he has done it, the result is something different from the original, and usually something less. In this case you will perhaps feel that the difference is to be found chiefly in the extraordinary eloquence of Barth. To have its full effect, this passage must be read eloquently, for it was written to be delivered as a lecture.

In this connection I would express the opinion that, generally speaking, German works when they are merely translated are not thereby perfectly adapted to the English reader. Besides a translation they need a transfiguration. This is not said in disparagement of the German way of putting things. Quite the contrary. I have wished, for example, that some of Friedrich Gogarten's books might be translated into English—yet in considering the possibility of doing this myself I have reflected that, though many of his published writings were delivered as public addresses to Christian youth, his argumentation is so subtle and closely knit that there might not be found in America even a select group which would have patience to follow him.

I pronounce again the opinion that the Barthian Theology will not be acclimatized in the English speaking world till original works in this *genre* are produced among us—which has been done lately by two Oxford scholars under the title *"Tell John."*

LECTURE III

THE KAIROS

The Arche

We have been considering the End, the *Telos*, and that prompts us to think of the Beginning. In the Bible it was the other way about. The fixed point was the Beginning, the *en arche* of the first verse of Genesis; and that prompted the men of the Bible to speculate more and more about the End. In reality, we cannot think seriously about the one without implying the other, and we cannot think wisely without constantly coordinating the End and the Beginning, as Barth does in the passage we have just read.

Looking back upon the early history of Christianity, it cannot but seem amazing that the Church maintained without wavering the doctrine of creation (creation out of nothing—that is, the absolute Beginning), in spite of the fact that it is an idea utterly foreign to Greek thought, which in other respects had so powerful an influence upon the development of Christian doctrine, and so seriously obscured the doctrine of the End. "Without wavering," and yet not without a terrible conflict. For essentially that is what was involved in the Gnostic controversy. It is ominous now to reflect how supinely we have suffered this hard won conquest to slip out of our hands. It has all been lost when we affirm that there is radically *no* qualitative difference between time and eternity.

Doubtless we may attribute this loss in part to the influence of science; for in our day we are not so much impressed by the authority of philosophy. But this means science *misunderstood;* for a science which understands itself does not presume to make any declarations about what lies beyond time and the limits of the material world. Yet even if science knew its limits better than it often does, its complete absorption in its proper field naturally enough creates the impression that beyond it there is nothing that could interest the human mind—or the human heart. But in fact the deepest interest of the human heart lies *beyond* the two thresholds which mark the confines of science—beyond the threshold of birth and beyond the threshold of death, *beyond* the Beginning and the End. It inquires anxiously whence life came, and still more anxiously whither it goes. That is, about the Source, which lies *before* the beginning, and about the Goal, the *Telos,* which comes *after* the end. So far as science is concerned, it seems now to be very significantly *pointing* to both these thresholds, though it cannot go beyond them. This is true at least of the triple alliance — physics-chemistry-astronomy — and there is reason to doubt if the others are *real* sciences. In this morning's paper I read that an eminent astronomer points decisively to the beginning of the material universe (the absolute beginning) . . . only about three billion years ago. Also the end is predicted—not of this or that star merely, but of all stars. But let Barth warn you (in the passage last read) that all this has little or nothing to do with the "last things"—or with the Source.

The myth of creation, as well as the eschatological myth, points emphatically *beyond* the threshold. The Book of Genesis does not mean merely *at* the beginning when it says "In the beginning." This is as clear

BEGINNING AND END

as can be in the first words of the Fourth Gospel ("In the Beginning was the Word"), which by this phrase announces itself as the Second Book of Genesis. Here "the Beginning" is evidently the Source, Eternity, God. Clearly, it would be false to say that the New Testament points to the End and the Old Testament to the Beginning. Genesis is a prophetical book—or else "By faith Abraham . . . by faith Isaac," and all the impressive catalogue in Hebrews 11 of men who pressed on with a comforted despair, looking for the city which hath the foundations, is mere rhetoric. How could there have failed to be, as St. Peter says, "prophets since the world began"—or at least from such time as man, "chucked into his whereabouts"[1] (as Heidegger significantly puts it), began to look up and ask, Whither? But it would be a far more serious mistake to say, as many are inclined to do, that the Old Testament looked forward merely to what was realized in the New—so that we as Christians have only to look *around* and try to make the best of this salvation which we *have*. The truth is that in the Old Testament the tension of expectation became ever more intense, and was most intense at the end, yet never *so* intense as the hope which Jesus prompted in his disciples. And on leaving them, his last injunction was, "Watch!" I repeat with entire conviction Barth's saying that "A Christianity which is not altogether and utterly eschatological has altogether and utterly nothing to do with Jesus Christ."

In this place I am chiefly intent upon the importance of having *both* ends in view. Even when we are most ardently pressing onward to the Goal we must not be unmindful of the Source. It is clearly the Biblical

---

[1] Geworfen in sein Da.

view that God is both the one and the other, both the Source and the Goal. The Revelation of St. John the Theologian (which is emphatically an eschatological book!) is not disposed to ignore the beginning even when it fixes attention upon the end. Jesus Christ is the Alpha as well as the Omega, the Beginning as well as the End. Scholars were over hasty in asserting, some time ago, that St. John's Gospel is not an eschatological book—notwithstanding the fact that it has such marked affinities with the Revelation. The impression it often gives that "eternal life" is a present possession, as if it were all that were ever coming to us, turns out to be a paradox: we have it and we do *not* have it. The mystic who relies upon this first impression is rudely startled by, "and I shall raise him up at the last day." In the Fourth Gospel Christ is very clearly the Beginning, but he is also the End—but the very End. He is not only the Way, but he is the Life at the end of the way. The initial and the final points are as securely fixed—and as clearly fixed *beyond* time—as anywhere else in the Bible. And that is all that is essential to eschatology.

These two points being fixed, a *line* is determined—a direction. Barth remarks that what is most characteristic of "the men of the Bible" is their "directedness." It requires *two* points to determine a direction. And mark you that if the line is to be an absolute one, the place where *we* happen to stand cannot serve as one of these points. A goal placed in front of us determines the direction we must take to reach it—if we have a mind to. But a line that is drawn between two fixed points, between the Source and the Goal, the Beginning and the End, the *Arche* and the *Telos*, has a very different sort of authority. It has the authority of absoluteness. In whatever direction *we* may go, and however far we may wander from that line, our position at every moment is determinable *with reference to it*. The men of the Bible were for the most part no better than we. But more or less clearly they had a sense of this line, a sense of directedness—even when they refused to be directed. We like to point the finger of scorn at Jacob, or David, or some other Biblical hero, and call attention to the fact that he was no *stinco di santo*—no shinbone of a saint, as the Italians say. Yet they were all better off than we are, in the fact that they had a sense of directedness. We cannot have that except as we keep the *Telos* in mind, except as we are essentially eschatologists. And yet there is a certain sense of directedness given by the thought of the finite end, our personal end, the death of the individual. That is at least an expressive parable of *the* End. But we have commonly given up even that determinant of direction. The Stoics were wiser than we because they did *not* refuse to have death in their knowledge and to reflect upon it. Those who are not oriented by the eschatological line which runs from Source to *Telos*, *i.e.* from Life to Life, do well to orient themselves by the line which runs from birth to death. It has not the same length, but it has (you may be surprised to note!) the same direction. The Preacher of the Book of Ecclesiastes makes that clear to us with his surprising exhortation: "Whatsoever thy hand findeth to do, do it with thy might; for there is no work, nor device, nor knowledge, nor wisdom in the grave whither thou goest." Christian ethics, the behaviour which Jesus enjoined upon his disciples, is not different (so Barth affirms) from the wisdom of Ecclesiastes, which is one of his favorite Biblical books. If Jesus had not given us *life* to think about, if he had not taught us to watch and wait for *that* with fear and trembling, he would have been even more express in teaching us to fear the ultimate death.[a] With that fear before our eyes we should be braver than we are, for we should be delivered by it from all petty fears; and we should be wiser than we are, if we were accustomed to refer every moment of our life to the end which so significantly qualifies it—if we would remember that we are mortal, as the Bible so eloquently and so constantly reminds us.

---

[a] Luke 12:4-12.

Between Two Worlds

We have come now to the central place of the Theology of Crisis. It is this *place* which justifies that name of crisis. I do not speak of it as a *point*, for what we here have to deal with is an *area*—the immense area which includes all time and all that exists in the time-form, which is the field of all our actions and the limit of our positive thought. And yet this "immense" area shrinks to mean proportions when we think of it as between two worlds and thereby are compelled to contrast it with eternity, with God. For remember that, if this is the central *place* of the Barthian Theology, the pivotal *point* of this theology is "the infinite qualitative difference between time and eternity." We must view this area in the light of that principle. This imposing area, therefore, has in itself no substantial importance: it is only an interval between two worlds. This phrase, "Between Two Worlds," is not a literal translation yet it is the most adequate rendering of *Zwischen den Zeiten,* the title adopted by the School of Crisis for its bimonthly theological review. We have already reflected upon a superficial suggestion of this significant title, but now we have reached the place where its deeper meaning becomes evident.

We cannot understand Barth's theology unless we recognize that his conception of this interval between two worlds which are qualitatively different from it radically excludes a monistic interpretation of the universe—to which the human reason by its very nature is prone, and to which the human heart is inclined by a guilty ambition to be like God,[8] or at least not absolutely, utterly, qualitatively different. This is the reason why Barth is suspicious of all philosophy, fearing monism even in Heidegger. And not without reason, for it is naturally the ambition of philosophy to explain everything with reference to a single principle. Dualism is the confession that this is impossible. It excludes the idealistic interpretation as well as the materialistic. But this tendency to resolve an evident dualism in a higher unity operates even in the philosophers who agree with the common opinion of today that monistic philosophy is discredited. About the dualism of the Biblical view of the world there can be no doubt, and if that is to be defended in its integrity, there will always be a controversy between philosophy and theology. It is just now "not a theory but a condition which confronts us," not a danger which threatens but a calamity which has already befallen us; and for the majority that has come not from the side of philosophy but of science, which is bound by its method and its aim to be, within its sphere, materialistically monistic. I merely call your attention here to a trait which we shall frequently encounter in Barth's polemic.

Recognizing where we are, *i.e.* in the interval between eternity behind us and eternity before, it is evident enough that we must exercise a certain amount of "intellectual asceticism." How can we know anything about what lies beyond this area, unless it be made known, that is, revealed to us? How can we speak of God and of eternity except in negative terms —or by parables which are confessedly inadequate? And even with regard to the things within this area, matters of experience, the objects of our senses, about

---
[8] The *eritis sicut Deus* of Gen. 3:5.

which we speak positively—how can we speak except in paradox, seeing that they are visible only in the weird light of this interval between two worlds and are not, we are compelled to suspect, what they seem? Even these things we cannot presume to understand apart from their Source and apart from the *Telos*.

When we say that we can speak positively about this present world, but only negatively about God and eternity, the meaning cannot be that in reality God and eternity are negative in contrast with the material universe. For we cannot put *this* world in contrast with the eternal world without making it appear profoundly negative. Nothing could be formally more negative than the *Nirvana* of Buddhist doctrine. Yet in contrast with the utter negativeness of this present world which all Gautama's logic was employed to prove, *Nirvana*, as the negation of this radical negation, may have been regarded as the ineffable fullness of positive reality. Rudolf Otto reports that a Buddhist replied to his question, What is Nirvana? with a beaming countenance and the confident answer, "Perfect bliss."

We must face the possibility that things as we see them in this present world are so far from being what they seem that they may even be the direct opposite. Gustav Theodor Fechner, who has had a great influence upon my thought, is clearly not a master through whom Barth traces his lineage. And yet Barth could not reject all of Fechner's analogies, provided they were regarded as parables. After all, it was Fechner who gave currency to the word "threshold" in the figurative sense in which Barth so much likes to use it. And in connection with the threshold one of Fechner's analogies seems to me not inappropriate to the Barthian theology. Looking at the threshold of birth from our point of view, standing between birth and death, it seems altogether a positive thing, the beginning of life; whereas when we look towards the threshold of death we can see nothing that is not negative—sheer destruction and dissolution. Yet to the unborn child the experience of birth is wholly negative, the severance of all the ties which bound it to its familiar world; and it may be that looking back upon death from the yon side it may appear as a birth. So far Fechner's analogy. Here I would apply it to the birth and death of the universe. Viewed from the Source, may not *the* beginning have been a *fall* from a higher realm of being? and if the destruction of the universe could be viewed in retrospect, might it not seem a birth?

Time, if it is not infinite, is limited at *both* ends by eternity—or by *Nirvana!* By the recognition of that fact time is qualified—not at the two ends only, but throughout. To say that time is finite means that every moment of time partakes of that negative quality. In that disparaging sense we commonly use the word *temporal*. And even without taking into account the absolute end, we recognize that change and decay are qualities of time.

Time is necessarily disparaged when it is viewed with reference to its end. The end must be regarded as a judgment upon time—a judgment of condemnation. And we are inclined to think of the end rather than the beginning, because we are commonly looking forward. Barth, at a time when he conceived that the contribution he was able to make was only "marginal notes," a "corrective theology," in short, a *protest*, dwelt predominantly upon the End as the qualification of time—rather than upon the Source. His protest against the prevailing doctrine of God's immanence in the world and every sort of disguised pantheism was so downright that it seemed as if he would separate this world altogether from God. And in spite of his attachment to the Old Testament, some of the Liberal leaders tried to fix upon him the stigma of Marcion's heresy—though two Apostles had used such hard phrases as, "the God of this world," and "the whole world lieth in the evil one." His colleagues have been more cautious, and his sympathizers have rightly insisted that this world must be viewed also with reference to its Source. As Creator, God surely has not allowed this world that he has made to slip entirely out of his hand. It is still his world, and he must feel its ruin as his loss. That, as Fechner says, is our firmest ground of hope; "for God has all means at his disposal, and all time." And considering how negative is this world in its time-form, how can we think of it as existing at all, except as it is supported by eternity. Eternity may be the substance of time. But here Barth warns us that if eternity be the substance of time, it is *concealed* in time. Brunner informs us that the word "distance" which Barth uses with so much emphasis is to be taken in an epistemological sense. Metaphysically God is not far. He created this world, and in him it exists. Yet God is *hidden* in this world—and chiefly for the reason that man on account of sin cannot see. Such warning is not unnecessary. It does not take much encouragement for men to vaunt their own divinity and the divinity of this world.

But a reference to its *Source* is not altogether flattering to the world. It is that which suggests the notion of a fall.

And the prospect of the End, if it is indeed regarded as the *Telos,* the goal and fulfillment of time, is anything but a reason for pessimism, even about the world as it is. The end, regarded merely as the termination of time, would not constitute a crisis. It would be merely a calamity, destined and inevitable. But the Theology of Crisis regards it as *the* Crisis. Crisis here means not simply a judgment of condemnation; it implies also the possibility of a happier outcome. The pessimistic view of the world as "vanity of vanities," which is not unreasonable in one who thinks of no end or, like Ecclesiastes, thinks of an endless succession of cycles, might be relieved (as in the case of Gautama Buddha) by the discovery of an end, but is lightened only by eschatology, *i.e.* the discovery of the End beyond the end—the resurrection of the dead. This does not constitute a crisis merely *at* the end, but is the crisis *of* the End—effective throughout the whole course of time, wherever the End casts its shadow, wherever eternity *makes* itself visible, wherever God speaks.

Barth would not speak, as Althaus does, of "the *permanent* shipwreck of time upon eternity."[4] He recognizes rather that certain times are peculiarly qualified by the End, by eternity. That is clearly the Biblical view. And that is the only view which makes the crisis real and acute, and an opportunity, involving a choice and exacting a decision prompt and resolute. It may be reasonable to think, speculatively, that apocalyptic (taking the word in its literal sense) means the *revelation* of the eternity which lies hidden in time. But at least we must strongly emphasize the word "hidden," for it is certain that the revelation of the Book of Revelation is conceived of as *entirely* future, not as the gradual manifestation of the immanent character of the universe, which might already be detected now and followed and fostered in its growth. On this point Bultmann is thoroughly in accord with the School of Crisis.[5] "*The kingdom of*

---
[4] *Die letzte Dinge.*

QUALIFIED TIME

God (God's rule) *thoroughly determines the present, although it is entirely future.* It determines the present by the fact that it compels men to make a decision. A man is defined thus or thus, as elect or reprobate, wholly and already in his present existence, by this decision. . . . God's kingdom is genuine future, since it is not a metaphysical entity, an inherent condition, but a future act of God which can be in no sense a present fact. Nevertheless this future determines man in his present, and is therefore genuine future (not a sometime and somewhere) because it is *coming* and forces man to a decision. The fact of the coming of the kingdom of God is therefore not properly a fact in the course of time, which some day will come, to which a man can if he will take a position, or remain neutral. But before a man takes a position a finger already points at him, and the question can only be whether he understands that his proper nature is to make decision. Because Jesus regarded men as put to the decision before God we can understand how the Jewish hope became to him the certainty that now is come the hour which ushers in God's rule. If man is put to the decision, and if it is this which characterizes him essentially as man, it is now and always the last hour; and we can understand that for Jesus the whole of contemporary mythology was of service to express this conception of human existence, and that he understood and proclaimed his hour as the last." The God of Jesus is a God of the future, yet he encounters us in our present. God is not only a God of the past ("the God of Abraham, the God of Isaac and the God of Jacob"[9]) but he encounters us out of the future where he is the guar-

---
[8] *Jesus*, pp. 49, 50, 143.
[9] Mark 12:24-27.

antor of our eternal life—and for this reason is our Judge in the present moment.

The whole scheme of the Fourth Gospel is determined, as everybody knows, by the conception that Jesus, as present among men, and by his every word and work, was their crisis, either for condemnation or for salvation. This is a just appreciation of an historical fact. The Synoptic Gospels, though they are not at all intent upon throwing this fact into relief, make it evident that Jesus did so conceive of himself, of his hour and of his message. With the only difference that they, more or less consistently, represent that Christ appeared among men "incognito," without being recognized as the Christ, and that his appearance was significant chiefly because he pointed to the End—*i.e.* to the kingdom of God and the Christ that was to come. One might suppose that when this critical moment was passed, and Christ was no longer here in the flesh, the crisis also would be passed and gone forever. That is to say, the opportunity for decision. (For the Last Judgment is *not* represented as such an opportunity.) Yet it was precisely *then* that the Apostolic witness insistently called men's attention to the fact that "*Now* is the acceptable time, *now* is the day of salvation."[7] It was a conception of the prophets that all times are not alike, and that it is God who makes them to differ, creating opportunities for men. Therefore Isaiah says, "Seek ye the Lord while he may be found, call upon him while he is near."[8] That is a conception which clearly justifies urgency. But Isaiah prophesied of a time to come which shall excel all such opportunities. He realized that he was sent expressly "to proclaim the

---
[7] 2 Cor. 6:2.
[8] Isa. 55:6; cf. Ps. 32:6; 69:13.

acceptable year of the Lord."[9] If Jesus fulfilled this prophecy, how could the Apostles apply it to later years without obscuring the distinctive thought that all times are not alike as opportunities—without admitting "the *permanent* shipwreck of time upon eternity?" They could do it because they did *not* preach Christ as the "historical Jesus"—could even show themselves indifferent to "Jesus according to the flesh." To use Kierkegaard's expression, they preached Christ as "contemporary." *That* is serious preaching, for that has the note of urgency. "Exhort one another today, so long as it is called 'Today.'"[10] For there is no knowing how long it may be called Today. Or whether any man will have such another hour of decision. Though the kingdom is always "near," even at the door!

The School of Crisis has learned from Kierkegaard to regard Christ as contemporary. And that puts everything in crisis! But a *real* crisis, which compels a decision. I said a moment ago, quoting Bultmann, that "the God of Jesus is a God of the future, but he encounters us in our present." That is to say, without in the least infringing upon the "distance," that God is contemporary. Of Christ also we must say that he is by no means a Christ of the past (of those long past few years in Palestine when he was not known to be the Christ, and in a sense was not *yet* the Christ—separated from us by the 18,000 years against which Kierkegaard protests), but he is the Christ of the future, the Christ who will come to be our Judge. But precisely in that character he encounters us now and here in our present, as our contemporary. In his earthly life Jesus emphatically pointed to himself, but to himself as the End, as the

---
[9] 61:2.
[10] Heb. 3:13.

Son of Man who was to come on the clouds to sit in judgment, like a shepherd when he separates the sheep from the goats. It is this that makes him so contemporary; and such contemporaneousness as this serves ever to fix our attention upon the End. We are no further from Christ than were the Christians of the first generation. He was their contemporary and is ours. Therefore with the same urgency we can proclaim that it is still called "Today." We can exhort one another, as sophisticated preachers for a long time have not ventured to do, because they were inhibited by the notion that in reality all times (artificial segments of *chronos*) and all moments of time are essentially alike. That is true enough of "Astronomer Royal time," but not of time which is more real than that because it is pure duration, and yet is disparaged as negative in contrast with eternity. Of that time we can say in sober reality that every part of it is not like every other, but that some moments are profoundly qualified by the fact that God speaks. We can say, therefore, with conviction, "Behold, *now* is the acceptable time; behold, *now* is the day of salvation." "Jesus Christ—yesterday, today the same, and forever."

As Source and Origin, God may be said to be contemporary. But that is to say a very different thing from that which we have just been saying. It means that a thrust out of the past is felt in the present through the sequence of cause and effect. The Jews recognized that in the Law God is present. In this case the analogy of physical causation does not perfectly apply. Nevertheless, it is as the past that God is present in the Law. Like all tradition, the Law means *pressure* from the past. This consideration leads us to reflect upon a feature I have till now ignored in dwelling upon the God of the future and the Christ of the future. I have hitherto dwelt solely upon the aspect of judgment, predominantly conceived in the sense of condemnation. But that is only one side; and a crisis, if it is a real crisis, must present an alternative. A threat may come out of the future, but also a promise. Properly speaking, neither can come out of the past. Out of the past can come only a thrust; out of the future, solicitation. So Paul says, "We are ambassadors on behalf of Christ, as though God were *entreating* by us." [11] The Gospel is, of course, far more a promise than a threat. But precisely because it is so entreating—"Come unto me, all ye that travail and are heavy laden"—because we are so lovingly bidden to the celestial banquet, is the condemnation of those who refuse (or simply decline to accept) the more absolute and the more condign. That is what it means to be "not under law but under grace." It is endlessly more critical. The "history of salvation" makes no sense, if it is only a story of the past and not also a story of the future. That is to say, if it is not eschatological. No one can fail to feel the passion in Jesus' reply to the Saducees, "Ye do greatly err! God is not a God of the dead but of the living." That means that God is contemporary—but our contemporary out of the future, *promising* the "resurrection of the dead." For that was the question at issue.

We find ourselves now in the area which is common not only to the school of Barth but to the much larger school of Kierkegaard. The key words we have been using, and some which I am about to use, are of his coinage and are distinctively characteristic of his thought. When we have said that Christ as "contemporary" constitutes "the Moment" [12] of "Crisis" which

[11] 1 Cor. 5:20.
[12] *The Moment* is the title of one of Kierkegaard's works.

sets us before the absolute alternative "Either-Or" and requires a prompt and resolute "Decision" of the will (that is, of the whole man), we have enumerated the fundamental themes not only of the School of Crisis and the Kairos Group which centers in Tillich, but of such detached thinkers as Unamuno and Heidegger—and I do not know how many others have been similarly influenced by Kierkegaard.

I have mentioned here for the first time the Kairos Group, but I have adopted the word *kairos* for the title of this chapter. The title of the Kairos Group means exactly what is meant by School of Crisis—unless it may be supposed to emphasize *opportunity* rather than judgment. I conceive that I am here presenting its central positions, which coincide at this point with those of the School of Crisis. I regret that I cannot quote much from Tillich, for he has important things to say and a striking way of saying them. But then I find as I go along that I have too little time to quote so much as I should like to do from Barth and his colleagues. The whole time is consumed by the task of presenting this theology schematically.[18]

At this point I conceive that I can best represent the school of Kierkegaard as a whole by speaking directly of that master. *Either-Or* was the title of the first great work Kierkegaard published (in two volumes). Though it ended with ethics and theology,

---

[18] I explain here my predilection for the word *kairos*. It does not, like *chronos*, mean clock time. One can speak of an "acceptable time", using *kairos*, but not in the same full sense with the use of *chronos*. For *kairos* means season, and is occasionally translated in the N. T. by "due season" and "due time". Twice it has to be translated by "opportunity", and that thought often lurks in it. Jesus can say, "My time is not yet full"; and St. Paul, "And that knowing the time." But that is always *kairos*, time in the critical sense, which expresses opportunity—for this ... *or* that.

it began with aesthetic criticism, for the sake of making appeal to a larger circle. The populace of Copenhagen did in fact bestow upon the author the title of this book as a nickname; but it was half a century before the resolute decision he required in the face of the most absolute of alternatives made a profound impression. His Either-Or was set in express opposition to the Both-And which Hegel had made acceptable by his discovery of the identity of contraries—which the Taoists had invented long before him. But the Both-And indicates not only the method of a philosophical school, but a *penchant* of the human heart to have one's cake and eat it too. The alternative Either-Or is therefore constantly stressed by Barth, who, though he is confronted no longer by an Hegelian philosophy, is aware of the general tendency of religion. It is this book which most obviously inspired Ibsen's *Brand*.[14] The Either-Or, when it involves the great alternative, God or the world, eternity or time, life or death, creates the "Moment." Barth commonly refers to it as "the existential moment," meaning thereby to indicate that it reveals a man's relatedness to the profound and constituent terms of his essential existence. Such a Moment calls for a decision which is sharp and instant and complete. A decision of the will—but that means of the whole man: intellect, feeling, muscles and marrow. This decision is the relief of "Anguish" (one of Kierkegaard's key words), and yet it remains founded upon anguish. It is an act of faith, and yet of a faith which continues to be founded upon doubt—yes, even upon despair, "a comforted despair." It is therefore anything but a meritorious faith. Barth makes this clear

---

[14] There are details which prove acquaintance with later books, although Ibsen is reported to have said that he had read little of Kierkegaard and understood less.

when in his *Romans* he persists, despite his critics, in translating *pistis theou* (which we render as "faith in God") as "the faithfulness of God." How can faith be meritorious if it is only trust in God's faithfulness?

There is only one principal term of Kierkegaard's vocabulary that is still unmentioned—it is the word *grace*. I make here a quotation to show how intimately he related grace to the other terms of this series.

" 'Grace' properly relates to that combination of temporalness and eternity which is man. When a body is too swiftly rotated on its axis it takes fire. So too when eternity and the requirements of ideality fall in an instant upon a man with their demand, he must despair, lose his reason *etc*. In such a moment a man must cry to God, Give time! give time! And that is 'grace'—So even the course of time is called grace-time (Gnadenzeit). In eternity there can be no such thing as grace, properly speaking. But the time-form is actually in a certain sense torment—and yet, divinely, it is grace-time."

I hope I have been able to make you see where the dynamic of the Barthian preaching lies. If so, though I have furnished you with no selection of texts for your sermons, and least of all the material needed for making them, you are in a position to make, not only your own Barthian theology, but your own Barthian sermons. The distinguishing *note,* as you cannot have failed to observe, of the Barthian sermon is urgency. Desperate urgency—and yet heartening, for it holds out not merely a threat but a promise. Who does not recognize that this note is commonly lacking in our sermons? Perhaps the people on hearing a note so unexpected might be more inclined to laugh than to cry . . . but perhaps not. One thing at least is certain, that the preacher himself, if he has no sense of the *authority* of his message, will not be able to preach urgently—except perhaps histrionically, if he is an accomplished actor. And where are we to seek the "seat of authority?" It has been made very plain to us that "the seat of authority in *religion*" is in the human heart. That being so, the preacher of religion has no reply to the man in the pew who asserts, "My think is as good as your think." But on the other hand it is no less plain that the men of the Bible did not expect to find the authority which was to govern their faith and their actions in the human heart—in the common experiences of religion, or even in the deepest mystical experience, but in the Word of God, in a "Thus saith the Lord." It is plain that the men of the New Testament looked for authority to the Old Testament. And that all generations of Christians who have followed them, up almost to our day, regarded the whole Bible as authority. That the Bible *is* the Word of God is still a part of the priest's vow, and the most substantial part of it. Nevertheless, there can be no doubt that this vow is generally made in a Pickwickian sense—because men feel that they *can* make it in no real sense. Since some authority must be had, we look for it in the Church. But from our modern point of view that can only mean a broad consensus of religious experience. Or else it means something which is neither very modern nor yet ancient enough to be found in the origin of Christianity—the notion, namely, that certain assemblies of men in councils held long ago were plenarily inspired to pronounce the truth. But compared to that how modest (I might say, how cautiously rationalistic) is the claim for papal infallibility! It is at least easier to think that *one* might be inspired, rather than many;

and easier still when no positive inspiration is asserted, no fullness of revelation of truth, but only the presumption that this *one* will be withheld (how negative!) from pronouncing error—when (if ever?) he speaks *ex cathedra* to the whole Church. That men grasp at this straw proves how necessary is authority for the preaching of the Gospel.

Kierkegaard knew the necessity of "authority." That was one of his key words. He knew that it must be *absolute* authority. Absolute or unconditional was another of his key words. And by that he did *not* mean the Absolute of Idealistic Philosophy. But the question of authority was no problem to him. He was a Fundamentalist in a day when almost all Christians were. He dealt with the Bible simply as the Word of God. If you know anything about Barth and the School of Crisis, you know that they are equally positive in looking to the Bible as authority and in seeking there the Word of God. You may well wonder how that can be, seeing that they have no quarrel with Biblical criticism, and that some (like Bultmann) carry it to an extreme. But this is the subject of another chapter. I refer to it here only because I would have you note that the Barthian School conceives of the Bible as a permanent occasion of crisis, whether it is read or whether it is preached. But that means, only when God himself is *heard* speaking—when God speaks to the individual and so creates the existential moment, the absolute Either-Or which exacts a decision.

I conclude this chapter with a parable of Kierkegaard's, to show what he and his school mean, and must mean, by *unconditional* authority. It is the parable of the King's Coachman. He is commenting upon 1 Pet. 5:8, "Be sober, be watchful."[18]

"So we have seen that it is the unconditional alone that can make a man entirely sober. Let me show you this by a picture, and do not be disturbed if the parable does not seem dignified and worthy enough. It is chosen expressly to give you a truer impression of the matter. If you should ask a cart-driver, a cab-man, a postillion, or a liveryman, what is the use of the whip, they would all reply, "Of course it is to make the horse go." But ask the king's court-coachman why the driver needs the whip, and you will get the answer, "Principally to make the horse stand still." That is the difference between ordinary driving and good driving. Have you ever observed how the coachman of the king handles the whip? If not, I will describe it to you. He sits high on his raised seat, and because he sits so high he has the horses more thoroughly under control. But occasionally that is not enough, when it is a question of bringing the horses instantly to a stand-still. He raises himself in his seat and concentrates his whole vital force in the muscular arm which lifts the whip—now falls a lash! it was terrible! Generally one lash is enough. Sometimes the horse makes a desperate jump—another lash. And that is enough. The coachman settles down on his seat. But the horse? First a tremor passes through its whole body. It looks indeed as if this fiery, powerful creature could hardly support itself on its legs. That is the first. It was not so much

[18] *Zur Selbstprüfung der Gegenwart anbefohlen* (Recommended to this Age for Self-examination), vol. II of the Collected Works, Diederich's edition, pp. 88, 89. I say here once for all, that, not knowing Danish, I can do no better than give a translation of the German translation. It would hardly occur to me to feel humiliated by this confession, were it not for the observation that Unamuno evidently reads his Kierkegaard in the original.

the pain that made him tremble, as the fact that the coachman (as only the king's coachman can do) gave accent to the lash with all his might, put himself wholly in it, so that, not so much by the pain as by something else, the horse could divine from whom the lash came. Then began this trembling. Now it is only a slight shudder, but it is as if every muscle shuddered, every fiber. Now that is past—now the horse stands still, absolutely still. What was this? It received an impression of the absolute; hence it stands absolutely still. When a horse which the king's coachman drives stands still, that is not at all the same thing as when a cabhorse stands still; for this means merely that it is not going, which is far from being an art. In the first case the standing still is an act, an effort, the very greatest, and it is also the horse's highest art. And it stands absolutely still. Absolutely still! How shall I describe that? I will use another picture, which comes to the same point. We commonly speak of still weather—though there may well be a slight breeze or a gentle movement of the air, it is none the less still weather. But have you ever taken note of another sort of stillness? Before a thunder storm there occurs occasionally such a stillness. It is of an entirely different sort: not a leaf moves, not a breath of air; it is as if all nature stood still, while yet, almost unobservable, a slight shudder passes over everything. What signifies the absolute stillness of this almost unobservable shudder? It means that the absolute is on its way, the storm. In the same way the horse stands absolutely still after it has received the impression of the absolute, the unconditional.

"A while ago we were saying that the impression of the unconditional makes a man sober, entirely sober—and at the same time alert, as the Apostle remarks in our text (1 Pet. 5:8). Is not that horse a symbol of this? It received the impression of the unconditional, and became as it were entirely sober and alert. Perhaps it was a very young horse, and therefore needed the impression of the unconditional. Perhaps it was an oldish horse which now with age had become shrewd, was sober in its sense of the word, and hence was of the opinion that one must not push things 'beyond a certain point'—this thing of standing still, among others, so that one need not stand absolutely still, but may make one's self comfortable, because it is far too much of an effort to stand absolutely still. In any case, the royal coachman was of an entirely different opinion—he administered to him an impression of the unconditional. And that the king's coachman always does. As one ordinarily drives, one does not even snap the whip. From a cabman or a carter you do not get the right snap of the whip. This is a superfluous luxury when he can belabor the horse with the butt of the whip. The gentleman's coachman snaps the whip, especially when he is driving his master. And when the carriage is stopped he sits and cheers the horses with his whip-snapping. This means that he drives well—but the unconditional he does not express. The king's coachman does not snap the whip: he expresses the unconditional—his royal majesty must not be too obviously reminded that he is driving. He holds *himself* . . . unconditionally still. Then he comes home. He throws the reins to one side—at once the horses understand that 'he' is not driving any longer. Out come the grooms, and lo! the unconditional is over for the time being; one can cool off or make one's self comfortable in any way one pleases; one need not be any longer on one's mettle, entirely his proper self, entirely sober—the unconditional is over for the time being.

"For it is only the unconditional that makes one entirely sober.

"But that surely is what we all are—entirely sober! Have we not all of us received the impression of the unconditional? the unconditional impression of the unconditional? For what is Christianity? Christianity is the unconditional—and we are surely all of us Christians! And what does it mean then to proclaim Christianity? It means to proclaim the unconditional. And we have in fact in Denmark a thousand parsons."

LECTURE IV

GOD

We began this study with an introduction which, though it brought into view all the Barthian themes, presented them only in a negative aspect, as a protest against current ways of thinking. In the second lecture we came abruptly upon the principle which characterizes this theology both as a theology of crisis and as a dialectical theology, namely, the infinite qualitative difference between time and eternity, between the world and God. With that we found ourselves in the central area of this theology, "between two worlds," and we dealt with the problems of this present world as they are qualified by the End and the Beginning. Now we come to the *meaning* of all this, which is God.

Not that God has been ignored in everything that has hitherto been said, but *now* this is the theme upon which our whole attention is to be fixed. We have talked of crisis; and it is evident that apart from God there can be no real crisis, no unconditional Either-Or, no absolute alternative, no challenge to the radical decision for all or nothing. Without God there is despair, but no "comforted despair." Man's "sickness unto death" (a phrase of Kierkegaard's which furnishes the title for one of his books) has no prospect of relief until it reaches its crisis; and this crisis is God. But I ask you to note that not every god is capable of putting us in crisis, but only the God who is God. For there are gods many, or rather, there are many ideas of God which have no tendency to challenge man or the world. Evidently the gods of philosophy cannot do it—whether it be the First Cause of the ancient physicists, or the *élan vital* suggested by biology, or the Absolute of the Idealists. It goes without saying that the Supreme Being of the Deists, remote and indifferent, does not challenge anybody. But neither do the gods of religion. Either they are too much involved in the world to be against it—they are *particeps criminis*—or they are too deeply and intimately related to man to put him in crisis. The God of the mystic which is discoverable *in* man might be said to put him in permanent crisis, but a permanent crisis is in reality no crisis at all. Only the God who is God is man's real crisis, only the living God who is not merely another word for life, the personal God who with respect to man and human personality is "the altogether Other"—to use Barth's favorite phrase.

I have spoken of God as the *meaning* of all the problems we have been considering. I would emphatically direct your attention to the word "meaning." You must note that it has nothing whatever to do with the word "value" which we have lately been accustomed to operate with. In the comparative study of religions we properly enough consider the "value" of this or that idea of God. We mean of course the value to man. It is not so evident that we can properly speak of the value of *our* God. A God whom we can think of as existing chiefly as a value to us is certainly not God. Ritschl encouraged us to content ourselves with "value judgments" about the great facts of the Christian faith, as a way of avoiding the critical inquiry whether they were true in a real sense. You must note that this all belongs in the philosophy of pragmatism, which affects to believe what it is good to believe, to accept as true whatever "works"—to use William James' brutal term. But that sort of believing is not faith, it is only "make believe." It is properly described by Vaihinger as "The Philosophy of As If."[1] This is the title of his work, which is much more thoroughgoing than any English or American Pragmatism, and for that reason it serves as a *reductio ad absurdum* of this whole type of thought, which is now so generally repudiated in Germany that in recent works you will rarely find the word "value" playing the rôle we still commonly ascribe to it. The philosophies which are now in the ascendent[2] claim that the human mind is not altogether incapable of knowing truth, and encourage us to seek no longer merely for "value" but for "meaning." When this idea was timidly proposed in England it was cruelly strangled at birth by an Oxford don who affected to examine "The Meaning of Meaning" (that is the title of his book) and came to the conclusion that the meaning of meaning is value. Which is the same as to say that meaning has no meaning. Here, however, where we are studying the Theology of Crisis, you are to understand that meaning is supposed to have a meaning, and that meaning is the thing chiefly sought after. In particular, God is understood to be the meaning of all the great facts we are here required to consider.

The accent of the Barthian theology (and this is true of the whole school of Kierkegaard) falls emphatically upon God. That "God is God" is the assertion Barth is never tired of repeating. It is the *leitmotiv* of his theology. This is the fundamental

---
[1] Hans Vaihinger, *Die Philosophie des Als Ob*.
[2] *E.g.* Edmund Husserl, *Logische Untersuchungen*, 3 vols.

creed which is shouted from all the minarets of Islam.
It needs to be shouted no less loudly from all the
pulpits of Christendom.

In my first lecture I remarked upon the complaint
that, try as we may, we do not succeed in pronouncing
the name of God with the ring it ought to have and
used to have. Neither strength of voice, nor variety
of intonation, nor any accent or emphasis we can con-
trive—whether we say Gawd or Almighty-God, as
different schools prefer—avails in the least to make
the name sound numinous. This suggests a disquieting doubt whether we really "believe in the divinity
of God." We have indeed reason to heed Barth's
warning and enquire seriously whether the God we
talk about and the God we worship may not turn out
to be the "not-God."

When Barth speaks of God as "the Other" we have
to understand this, first of all, as a polemic against
the views of God we commonly hold. More radically
understood, God is "other" than even the highest
ideas we as religious men can possibly entertain of
him. However noble our notion of God may be, and
however useful or necessary, we must say to ourselves,
This is *not* He; we must check ourselves constantly
by the reminder, "How much more!" Gogarten, perhaps because of his Lutheran antecedents, is more
interested than Barth in anthropology and defines even
more sharply than he the limits of human understanding.[1] Yet Barth also insists that the true God is the
"unknown God." And he evidently means more than
this when he speaks of God as "the absolutely Other."
He means that God is other than man, other than the
world—but *absolutely* other, *the* Other.

This is by no means an unnecessary assertion in our
day. Barth properly feels that one of the most serious

---

[1] But see Brunner, *Die Grenzen der Humanität*, Mohr, 1922.

things we have to do is to "reinstate the distance" between God and man. It is not that God has come too close to *us*, in that "nearness" which we rightly apprehend in Jesus Christ, but that *we* press up insolently too close to God. That is man's *hybris*. It is not a spacial distance between God and the world that Barth has in mind; for that is something we could make neither greater nor less, however earnestly we were exhorted to do it. Our own temerity, however, in approaching too near to God and approaching too familiarly we *can* restrain. We are warned not to fraternize with God, who is Father—and the Father in *heaven*.

The exhortation to "reinstate the distance" is connected with the Barthian polemic against the practice of mysticism, the doctrine of immanence, and reliance upon religious experience. That is to say, against all the things which are most highly esteemed in our religious world of today. That must disconcert us—if it does not rather render us indignant. And yet it need not surprise us. Plainly something serious needs to be done, if in fact our plight is so grave as I have suggested—if we can no longer utter the name of God in such a way that it is even religiously effective. And if this disturbing fact is a new symptom, one which was not manifested in the generations immediately preceding us, it cannot seem improbable that the causes of it are to be sought precisely in the influences which are now predominant in the Church. I say "in the Church" rather than in the world, because the enemy within the fortress is always more dangerous than the enemy without. A few years ago the Jerusalem Missionary Conference detected and named the enemy. It is "secularism." But that is only another name for worldliness, the spirit of this world. And this spirit is not easily kept out of the Church. It appears there in its most insidious disguise when the world is confounded with God and God with the world. To "reinstate the distance" means to liberate God from this entanglement.

The doctrine of divine immanence *begins* as theism, but only too readily it merges into pantheism. We think that we have insured the integrity of our theism when we assert that God, though he is more or less manifestly immanent in all the world, must be believed to transcend it all.

> They are but broken lights of Thee,
> And Thou, O Lord, art more than they.

If we venture to say such things, at least we must not for one moment forget that we are on a slippery slope. But perhaps already we have slipped too far. Barth is not contending against possible or imaginary dangers. He contends against the notion of immanence as it is now actually held within the Church and by theists. The position he attacks is not that which makes the world conterminous with God, but that which regards the world as the luminous revelation of God, rather than as the cloak which *hides* the Godhead. He addresses us who detect no paradox in St. Paul's assertion that "the invisible things of God are visible in his works—even his eternal power and Godhead!"

At this point I interject a short passage from Barth's *Romans,* both because it is appropriate here, and because you ought to hear a sample of this famous commentary. I translate his comment upon Rom. 1:20: "For from the creation of the world until now, the invisible things of God—even his eternal power and Godhead!—are visible to intelligent perception." So he translates.

"God's 'invisibility is visible.' We have forgotten

that, and must suffer it to be told us again. It is not necessarily involved in the situation as between God and us that our impudence, nonchalance and fearlessness over against him should be so natural to us. Platonic wisdom recognized long ago that the Source of all that is 'given' is the 'not-given.' Sober worldly wisdom long ago concluded that the fear of the Lord is the beginning of knowledge. Open and undimmed eyes like those of the poet Job and the Preacher Solomon long ago rediscovered in the mirror of intuitive vision the archetype, the invisible, the unsearchable majesty of God. Ever is the voice of the Lord perceptible in the thunder storm, ever prompting us to the recognition that we speak unadvisedly with our lips when we talk of that which is too high for us and beyond our understanding, when as God's advocates or as his accusers we argue a case with him as if he were of our own kind. There ever lies before us like an open text-book the problematic of our existence and of such an existence as it is,[4] the vanity, the utter questionableness, of all that is and all that we are. What else then are God's *'works'* in their absolutely enigmatical strangeness (zoological garden!)[5] but sheer questions, to which there is no direct answer, to which God alone, only God himself is the answer? The divine 'No,' which intimates our limits and at the

---

[4] Da-Seins und So-Seins.
[5] The allusion is to Rudolf Otto's *Idea of the Holy*, where the fierce stallion, yes, and behemoth and leviathan (crocodile and hippopotamus), are recognized as revelations to Job (oh, how indirect!) of the character of God. And perhaps reflecting also upon the human characters depicted by Dostoiewski, of which Thurneysen, in his book entitled *Dostojewski*, has said that returning from them to the tame of the same species is like seeing the family cat with a fresh eye on returning from a menagerie where we have viewed with astonishment tigers and lions and other wild felines. We are prompted to think of Blake's enigma: "Tyger, tyger, gleaming bright . . . Did he who made the lamb make thee?"

same time points beyond them, can, 'from the creation of the world until now, be in his works intelligently perceived,' can by a quiet, factual, unprejudiced religious view be detected and understood. Nothing can hinder the thought of God from producing in us a health-bringing crisis, unless we ourselves hinder it. We already find ourselves in such a crisis, if only we are willing to 'intelligently perceive.' And what to 'intelligent perception' has ever been unquestionable fact, namely, God's invisibility, just that, in agreement with the Gospel of the resurrection of the dead, constitutes God's 'eternal power and Godhead.' Precisely that. That we can know nothing of God, that we are not God, that the Lord is to be feared, *that* is his preëminence above all other Gods, that it is which characterizes him as God, as Creator and Saviour (Rom. 1:16). The line which separates time and eternity, this present world from the world (1:4) to come, runs in fact through the whole of history; it was 'long ago proclaimed' (1:2), it could always be seen. Not as an inevitable doom was the wrath of God disclosed against the men who stand before his judgment: they could acknowledge the Judge and love him. 'So that they have no excuse,' if they do not see and do not hear, what requires only seeing eyes and hearing ears. Their irreverence is inexcusable; for the 'intelligently perceived' works of God speak of his '*eternal* power' and protest in advance against the service of the known not-God, through whom God is associated with the natural, psychical and other powers of this world. Inexcusable is also their disobedience, for the 'intelligently perceived' facts testify to the '*eternal* Godhead' of God and protest in advance against the religious temerity which in the giddy exaltation of its experiences talks of God and means itself.—If we have 'held down' and put a lid on the truth of God, and thereby challenged his wrath, we cannot say that no other possibility was open to us. 'God is not far from every one of us, for in him we live and move and are' (Acts 17:27-28). The situation might have been different, so far as he is concerned."

It is clear from these last words that the "distance" Barth so much insists upon was never thought of as spacial remoteness; but it is clear also from the whole passage that the task of reinstating the distance, as he conceives it, is one of immense difficulty and of supreme importance.

I have spoken of the "theory" of immanence and of the "practice" of mysticism. And this distinction is not inappropriate. For immanence is first of all a theory, though we may be said to practice it when we press up too close to God. And mysticism is first of all a practice, although the multitudes in Europe and America who are loud in extolling the mystical way with no thought of treading so arduous a path, are for the most part not presumptuous enough to call themselves mystics or to claim a mystical experience, but are content to contemplate the obscure report which others attempt to make of their ineffable visions. It is chiefly against such pseudo-mystics Barth drops his scornful word. To them a rational appeal can be made, inasmuch as it is only a theory and a value-judgment they cherish, not a practice. From the value-judgment which accounts the mystical way the most sublime of all the "varieties of religious experience" Barth would hardly dissent. But religion *as a whole*, with all its expressions and experiences, even the sublimest, he would cheerfully relegate to the province of psychology and to the none too tender mercies of the psychologists. He has no more interest in religion than the Bible has, which never mentions the word except to disparage it.

But because the prevalent interest in mysticism is the expression of a theory, it cannot be ignored by one who, like Barth, is interested in faith and revelation —in faith, that is to say, as the response to an objective revelation. For mysticism implies another faith, a most subjective faith, that in the depths of human nature, if one will take the pains to delve so far, not only can we discover more and more of man, but finally . . . God! Such a faith renders faith in an objective revelation superfluous. The title of one of Brunner's books, *Mysticism and the Word*[6] shows in what interest the warfare against mysticism is waged. Mysticism is an *alternative* to revelation conceived as rational and intelligible speech. But this alternative also implies that God does not call and seek and find us—that rather it is we who are active and successful in seeking and finding and seeing and hearing God, even though he makes no move to approach us, or to manifest himself, or to speak to us.

I am one of those that are "interested" in mysticism and in the great mystics. But I am interested as a psychologist; and the observation that all mystics, whether they be Protestant or Catholic or pagan, have an identical experience and formulate it in much the same terms, inhibits me from thinking that mysticism has any positive contribution to make to the Christian faith.

It is interesting to note that St. Paul had one extraordinary mystical experience,[7] although few have ever thought of classing him among the great mystics. But is it interesting also to observe that upon this experience he presumed to found nothing: and that

---
[6] Die Mystik und das Wort, 1924.
[7] 2 Cor. 12:1-4.

Christ's appearance to him, upon which he founded everything, he emphatically did not regard as a mystical experience. It is noteworthy that he commonly uses mystical expressions, such as "in" and "into" Christ Jesus; but it is equally noteworthy that, as Albert Schweitzer points out,[8] his Christ-mysticism was never expressed as God-mysticism, that he did not ignore the "distance" between man and God when he believed himself to be in touch with "the Lord who is the spirit."[9] And we must note moreover that "in Christ" is a phrase which does not indicate a religious experience, or anything at all that can be treated as a phenomenon, upon which one might build one's faith, but indicates something which is *not* experienced, which is altogether "hid,"[10] which is only to be apprehended by faith. About the Johannine writings, I have already raised the question whether they are mystical in any other sense than this, and do actually exclude eschatology. It can be said confidently about the Apocalypse that its preoccupation with the End, and in particular the conception that *after* the End there will be no Temple needed, because *then* "the Lord God and the Lamb are the Temple thereof,"[11] excludes any thought of mystical union with God *now*. In the Bible the thought of the "then" is always disparaging to the "now." It would appear indeed as if temples were regarded here as a symbol of God's distance. And, in fact, when we apply to our churches the wondering exclamation of Jacob, "This is the *gate of heaven!*" we intimate (inadvertently perhaps) that our temples are planted exactly on the threshold between time and eternity as a solemn *reminder* that

---

[8] *Die Mystik des Apostles Paulus*, 1930.
[9] 2 Cor. 3:17.
[10] Col. 3:3.
[11] Rev. 21:22.

"God is in heaven, we on earth." And so far as concerns the other writings that bear the name of John, the conclusion of the First Epistle makes it plain that the confidence that "*we* are of God" is founded on Christ-mysticism ("we are in him that is true, in his Son Jesus Christ"), and the devastating assertion that "the whole world lieth in the evil one" excludes for man the possibility of any other mysticism. Which is evident also in the Gospel, where the Beginning is so much stressed, and where the Word coming out of that Source is apprehended only as He is *believed*, and is the only Way to the Father. But chiefly I would call attention to St. Paul's emphatic recognition of the present "distance" when he declares to our amazement that *only* in the End will God be "all and in all."

It would be an excess of zeal if the Barthian polemic were levelled against the few authentic mystics there ever have been in the world; but as against the common presumption that mysticism is the normal way of coming to God it is very much in place. Still more against the pretention, so discouraging to many, that no one who lacks a mystical disposition (or as we say more commonly, a religious temperament) can have any dealings with God. We must recognize that there is nothing in the Bible to suggest, either that the possession of a religious temperament is a key to the kingdom of God, or that the lack of it is any impediment to entrance therein. It is significant that Jesus found his adherents chiefly among "irreligious" people—for that is properly the meaning of the word we translate by "sinners" in the Gospels.

In fact, Barth's polemic is not directed against one sort of religious experience rather than another, but against the assumption that religious experience of any sort is a way to God—that by our experiences the existence of God can be proved or his character known, or our relation to him attested. This is the field of the Barthian polemic against Schleiermacher, and against pretty much everything that is characteristic of modern theology.

This challenge is disconcerting to us, for we have all become Methodists without meaning to. Yet we cannot summarily dismiss it, for it clearly applies to us—especially now when we are uneasily aware how ineffective our religion of experience has proved. We can hardly disguise from ourselves the fact that we sought refuge in "experience" because we were fearful lest the object of our faith might turn out to be unreal. *Real*—often too crassly real—is religion and religious experience. For a moment we were flattered to observe that psychologists (even atheistical psychologists) regarded religion as worthy of attention and treated it as a reality. Both the opponents and the defenders of Christianity were intent upon the study of this interesting phenomenon. Both sought to explain it, and both necessarily explained it away. For to conclude that it could be explained completely as a soulish phenomenon (or do you prefer to say psychic?) was to concede that it is not what it takes itself to be, that is to say, not a spiritual phenomenon (as though there could be such a thing!), not a foundation for faith in God and eternity, but at the very most a *product* of faith. In the pass to which we now have come you might not be disinclined to listen to the Barthian polemic against "psychologism," and be willing almost to sacrifice religion, if only our faith might be rescued from the psychologists. But I have no time to follow any further the polemic against psychology-out-of-its-place. As for the faith, we shall see in the sixth lecture that it is effectually delivered from the psychologists when it is referred to revelation.

But if God is not revealed in the heart of man, in human nature, neither is he revealed directly in the amazing world of life below man, nor in the realm of inanimate nature. Barth's assertion that God is rather hidden than revealed in nature is exactly contrary to our familiar belief. A belief we desperately cling to, even when we are reminded (perhaps with some exaggeration)

> That Nature red in tooth and claw
> With ravin shrieks against our creed;

even though it involves us in endless perplexities, and even though it embroils us in a conflict with science. For theistic scientists are most of them as clear as are any others about the fact that God is not directly discoverable in nature. And philosophers now agree with the scientists in discrediting the argument from nature to the existence of God. Being in this plight, it would seem as if we might be ready to welcome deliverance from all these vain conflicts—even at the cost of accepting Barth's dictum that God is "the unknown God." This is the last term of the "distance" Barth so much insists upon. But even here you are to remark that it is not virtual separation from God he asserts, but a distance which inspires reverent awe for the "God who dwelleth in light unapproachable and full of glory"; and that while he excludes the possibility that across such a "distance" (which is no measurable distance at all, but only the hair-line between time and eternity) we might discover God for ourselves, he emphatically does not exclude the possibility that God might speak to us across this "distance" by a word of truth and righteousness. His assertion is that "there is *no* way from man to God,

THE TRANSCENDENT GOD

but only from God to man." This lapidary phrase is the motto of all his theology. It casts down our presumption, only to raise us up again by the prospect of God's help. We shall not be looking for that help so long as we are confident of being able to help ourselves. We do not give God the glory which is his due so long as we claim any credit for our own salvation. The motto of the School of Crisis is the old Reformed motto: To God be all the glory.

"No way from man to God," means that even religion, though it is meant as an approach to God, is *not* a way by which we can reach him. It is a Tower of Babel, testifying only to man's presumptuous and vain desire to "scale the steep ascent of heaven." God it would seem has again effectually balked that attempt by the confusion of tongues. Even in Christendom we do not find it possible to build up a concordant faith upon the basis of a great variety of religious experiences. Barth is of the opinion that agreement upon a common creed, even for Protestant Christendom, is not a possibility in our day, and that before such a thing can wisely be attempted long and laborious theological study will be necessary.

"No way from man to God," means also that God absolutely transcends our understanding. Not even a proof of his existence is possible to us. Barth sweeps away with scorn the whole apparatus of apologetic for theism. Brunner says trenchantly that "*next* to the foolishness of denying God, certainly the *greatest* is that of proving him." This, of course, is not a position peculiar to the School of Crisis. And Tillich[11] remarks that "it has the great advantage of putting an end to all efforts to argue from the finite and its forms to the infinite and eternal. It makes it

---
[11] *Die religiöse Lage der Gegenwart*, p. 140.

impossible to use the incompleteness of scientific knowledge as an opportunity to propose God as a stop-gap for the lacunae of the scientific world-view. It confirms the conclusion that the eternal manifests itself in a deeper stratum than that of rational thought. But on the other hand, by the fact that this deeper stratum was described as feeling, which could be brought into no relation with the scientific view of the world, the whole sphere of truth, divorced from religion, was left to itself and to its own finite realization. While religion for its part was treated as a subjective disposition which could make no claim to influence the world and mould it."

The distinction of the Theology of Crisis is that it has not been brought to this position by discouragement, by the failure of all efforts to argue from the world to God, but radically excludes a priori all such effort by its assertion of the infinite qualitative difference between time and eternity. It is easy to see how this principle excludes the notion of "natural law in the spiritual world," if that is taken to mean continuous development, uninterrupted by the line which separates time and eternity. At the most, nature and natural law can be no more than a parable of the other world. The teleology which presumes to see

> That all as in a piece of art
> Is toil coöperant to an end

can refer only to an end which is before *the* End. For the destiny of *this* world is simply to *end*. And with regard to *this* world, not even the few scientists who look up from their specialties to take a broad view are bold enough to declare that they perceive a plan of the whole or see anything but finite purposes of the creatures conflicting with one another. Nor would it be reasonable to expect to perceive the wholeness of the universe before the end.

> The one far off divine event
> Towards which the whole creation moves,

though it is surely in God's purpose and in God's power, may not be so "divine" as the evolutionist poet imagines it; for *beyond* this end lies the true *Telos*, the kingdom of God.

For my part, I am not rendered disconsolate by the apprehension that I cannot see God in the world, except—so indirectly!—in the thunderstorm, in leviathan and in behemoth. We are not necessarily reduced to the position of Darwin when he piteously confessed that he could no longer perceive any beauty in the world *because* he saw so clearly the purpose of every detail, that is to say, its usefulness. I have learned from Fries[18] not to disparage beauty and sublimity in nature, but to feel in them "a presentiment of the eternal in the temporal." A presentiment only —"fallings from us, vanishings," is Wordsworth's perfect phrase. Fries recognizes that we are incapable of passing by a logical judgment from individual purposes to the purpose of the whole. The presentiment he remarks upon is aroused by the contemplation of the sheer beauty of individual objects, a free combination of parts which produces a pleasurable impression of harmony and wholeness in one who regards it with "favor" and without any reference to utility. Beauty and sublimity in nature are here valued as something more than a parable, inasmuch as they directly prompt a presentiment of eternity. And I have learned from Fechner to argue by analogy from the wholeness of

---

[18] Neo-Kantian philosopher, whose most important work, *Wissen, Glaube und Ahndung*, was published in 1805 and again a century later precisely. I refer especially to pp. 176, 177, 182, 220, 223.

individual living forms to the wholeness of the whole. And it is amazing to me that General Smuts, in his book strangely entitled *Holism and Evolution,* though by his recognition of the wholeness of living beings (and of "wholeness itself as an active factor") he transcends mechanical materialism, does not conceive that the wholeness of the parts might prompt even a presentiment of the wholeness of the whole. In the end it becomes evident that, because he does not regard the All as a Whole, he cannot seriously treat the wholeness of the individual as "an active factor" (*i.e.* as soul), but only as a "concept."

I see no reason to suppose that the much talked of "lillies of the field" were for Jesus a clear mirror in which he could see the Father in heaven, or furnished anything more than a presentiment of the eternal in the temporal. It is appropriate that you should ask yourself here whether the notion of "distance" which we have been dwelling upon is or is not the notion of the Bible. There can be no doubt that the God of the Old Testament was a transcendent God. "Verily, thou art a God that hidest thyself, O God of Israel, our Saviour," Isa. 45:15. In our generation this fact is not only conceded but is regarded as highly disparaging to the "Jewish Bible." But in the New Testament there is a new note which is even more disquieting. It finds its extremest expression in such phrases as, "the God of *this* world," and "the whole world lieth in the evil one." I would have you observe, however, that this does *not* imply the late Greek notion of the demiurge, nor the medieval notion (tinged with Persian dualism) which regards the devil as a power which shares the regiment of this world with God. It means something *more* radical than that. For the New Testament makes it plain that in no part of this fallen world—not even in human nature, nor even in the society of elect sinners—can we expect to discover one spot which mirrors the glory of the eternal God.

The profession that God is the "unknown God" is not a disconsolate one. It means the destruction of many idols—to open the way for God's revelation of himself. It means the despair of finding God—unless he has first found us. It means the denial of all human possibilities—in order to make way for God's possibility. It means that "there is no way from man to God"—but in the same breath it affirms, "only from God to man." It abases all human imaginations—in order to make room for the Names by which God proclaims himself, and especially for his new Name as "the God and Father of our Lord and Saviour Jesus Christ."—That is the subject of the next lecture.

In conclusion I quote a passage from Brunner's principal work,[14] *Mysticism and the Word,* which, although it is a polemic against Schleiermacher, applies punctually to us. In part, as you will see, it deals with the themes we have been considering in this lecture, and what goes beyond this will serve as an introduction to the two lectures which follow.

Brunner says of the Reformers, "it was not the pathos of distance as posited by the mystics which was abhorrent to *them,* not the difficulties of the 'way,' the pains involved in the threefold (or sevenfold) death. On the contrary, what *they* protested against was the fact that these distances were not taken seriously enough, that these obstacles were of a sort that man *could* at last succeed in overcoming (if he would take the pains), that eventually he could attain the *theologia gloriae* (*habemus Deum*), that in spite of all the

---
[14] *Die Mystik und das Wort,* pp. 186 ff.

mystical deaths the old Adam who desires to be as God would not die, and could boast, with however humble a bearing, of being in possession of the divine secret of life, that *finally* (though after great effort) the dividing wall between God and man was sure to fall. This impiety, which is the common and essential note of mysticism and the philosophy of immanence, this daring to cross the border line and be at last one with God, this is what moved the Reformers to prophetic wrath. This *hybris*, more than all practical and moral corruptions, was what they intended when they spoke of the spirit of Antichrist in Rome. They meant the delusion, prompted by irreverence and presumption, that at least in our inmost part we are not depraved, that somewhere within us God dwells, that there is still a point—no, far more than a point!—a psychical area, an experience, a process, where God is man and man God, where the Creator is creature and the creature Creator, where our being coalesces with divine Being; that there is at least some fragment of human life which is not in need of forgiveness and salvation but simply *is*. It was precisely this mystical tendency, this tendency to psychologize what the spirit indeed *means* but does not possess, to which it indeed refers but cannot properly be said to be; the perversion of the Gospel attitude of aiming at, gazing towards, harkening for, into a possession and enjoyment —that is to say, precisely that in which Schleiermacher far exceeded all other philosophers of immanence, even to the insuperable perception that God is in us a *given fact*—precisely this false doctrine was the object of the Reformers' polemic. For this reason they put faith (*sola fide*) in a central position. For faith in God is the opposite to experience of God. To have faith in God, means that in spite of the absolute separation between man and God, which by no means can be abolished, or even be conceived of as abolished, least of all experienced as abolished; in spite of the fact that no way leads from man to God; in spite of the fact that there is no smallest point in the soul where man can be thought of as not far off from God and fallen (least of all in the innermost places of the heart); in spite of the fact that there is no experience, even the most blessed, which as human experience is at the same time divine—in spite of all this, faith apprehends that nevertheless we are, just as we are, with God united, because God so wills it. And we know it (in spite of the fact that it goes against all experience) because *God says so*. For that reason and only for that reason. *Against all experience* stands our faith, as it stands against death and the devil—against all the results of introspection, which, if it is honestly enough conducted, always looks fatal to us; against all that we experience, which, as *our* experiencing, is also ever and in every point affected by the fragility and godlessness of our existence; against not only all that we ourselves *think*, but against all that we ourselves can *will* or *feel*. Hence it is that God can only be believed, and that this faith is an inconceivably bold enterprise—yes, from the standpoint of experience, sheer madness. That is the clear witness of the Reformation."

LECTURE V

JESUS CHRIST

The subject of the last lecture was God, but *Deus absconditus*, the unknown God. The subject of this is *Deus revelatus*, God as he reveals himself in Jesus Christ. *God in Christ* seemed to me therefore the most obvious title for this lecture, and I proceeded to declare that it is evidently an "unambiguous" title. Unambiguous it is indeed! But I reflected at once that no title so unambiguous could be appropriate to this lecture, if here we are *really* to consider what is the meaning of the name Jesus Christ. For Jesus Christ is the most ambiguous, problematical, paradoxical name which has ever been pronounced by human lips.

I was reminded then of the difficulty of expounding *another* man's thought dialectically—even if it be the thought of a dialectical theologian. When we ask *ourselves* questions about God, or if we address our questions desperately to God himself, the situation is essentially dialectical, and we must often be content with hearing our own questions retorted to us as the answer. But in the case of anything so objective as a book, even the books of dialectical theologians, we are disposed to fix our attention upon the positive positions which they express or which they may be presumed to imply; and where we find nothing but paradox we are inclined to supply the synthesis. For that reason the expounders of the Barthian theology do not treat it fairly. Nor can I do it justice so long as I am merely an interpreter. But here at *this* point I am warned to take care when I note that Barth's pages nowhere glitter so dazzlingly with paradox as in the passages which deal with Jesus Christ.[1] And if in the *Dogmatics* the style is calmer, this is not because the essential paradox of the name Jesus Christ is ignored, or slurred over, or resolved, but only because the many paradoxes are treated as one.[2]

In this connection, it cannot but be instructive, as a way of approach to the Barthian theology, to consider how the theme *Jesus Christ* might be treated undialectically. Substantially, there are but two ways. And it is the more instructive to consider them because they are not hypothetical constructions of notions which people *might* entertain, but are the two different ways by which most of our contemporaries are disposed to resolve the paradox of the name Jesus Christ.

I do not say *three* ways, because the way of dealing with this name which still seems obvious to many simply ignores the paradox. It seemed perfectly possible until a short while ago to think of the word "Christ" as a title of human dignity. Did not Moses say, "A prophet shall the Lord God raise up unto you from among your brethren *like unto me?*" Could anything be less paradoxical than that? It is true, we recognized that Jesus of Nazareth did not exactly fulfill the "crude" expectations of what the Messiah would be. He was neither a lawgiver like Moses, nor a king like David, nor a nationalistic hero like Judas Machabeus. But this recognition merely prompted us to say that he was "greater than Jonah,

---

[1] *Romans,* pp. 5, 6, 66-81, 125-141, 182-187, 259-266.

[2] Pp. 214-229, 252-284. It is to be noted that this theme is dealt with here by anticipation, and only in so far as it has to do with Revelation, which is the theme of the *Prolegomena,* the only part of the *Dogmatik* which has yet appeared.

greater even than Solomon," by reason of a "genius for religion" which made him preëminent among all teachers of morals and religion, so that we can justly describe him as *the* Teacher, *the* Master. That we accounted a more "spiritual" idea of messiahship. But could anything be less paradoxical? This is the notion which is expressed in that greatest triumph of Liberal Theology, the construction which we know as the Life of Jesus. That was so imposing a construction that all the lives of Jesus which have been written by devout Christians for edification follow, more or less inconsistently, the lines of interpretation which it established.[3] That is no longer possible for those who know the times in which they are living. Suspicion was thrown upon this whole elaborate construction so soon as it was pointed out that Jesus himself (in his own "self-consciousness") attached to the title Son of Man a heavenly significance. This Son of Man is to come on the clouds of heaven to judge the world! If such was Jesus' own conception of what it means to be the Christ, we are confronted by a dilemma, which is in itself no paradox but may involve one: either Jesus was mad—*or else* he is a paradox. Albert Schweitzer not only uttered the dictum that the Liberal Lives are *not* historical and that such a figure as they depict never existed, but he proved it.[4] It ought not to be possible today for any man to avoid both the dilemma and the paradox.

The paradox in the name Jesus Christ was clearly

---

[3] On receiving from Bishop Gore the gracious gift of his little book *Jesus of Nazareth* I expressed to him churlishly my regret that his name would assure for it many readers, although substantially he depicted the Liberal Jesus.

[4] First in a book entitled *Das Abendmahl*, published in 1901, a part of which I translated, published under the title of *The Mystery of the Kingdom of God*, in 1914; 2nd ed. Black 1925. Then, in 1906, in his *Geschichte der Leben-Jesu-Forschung*, English trans. *The Quest of the Historical Jesus*, 1910.

recognized by the publication in 1909 of a supplementary volume of the Hibbert Journal with the title *Jesus or Christ*, in which seventeen well known scholars argued on different sides. But you will note that by the very title of this significant book the paradox was disclaimed by the very statement of it: Jesus *or* Christ. It was assumed that no one who knew what Christ meant could say Jesus *and* Christ. At that time, the heyday of Modernism, there seemed little doubt to which side of the alternative, Jesus *or* Christ, men of light and leading would incline. It is a curious coincidence that in that same year (1909) appeared Arthur Drews *Christusmythe,* the ultimate effect of which was to show how many there are who are far better satisfied to believe in the mythical Christ than in the "historical Jesus." But the mythical solution, because it also is a way of avoiding the paradox, need not be considered here.

The first way of dealing with the paradox is that which is illustrated by the saying with which Renan introduced his *Life of Jesus* (which I quote from memory and perhaps not exactly): "In the reign of Augustus there was born in Nazareth, a small town in Galilee, a man of so extraordinary a character that I have no quarrel with those who call him God." Here it is evident that the paradox is not radically conceived, for there would appear to be nothing more than a *quantitative* difference between time and eternity, between man and God, between the name Jesus and the title Christ. Nevertheless, the paradox is clearly enough stated. It could be stated no more sharply than this: A *man* called *God.* The fact is that Liberal Theology has not commonly been willing to state it so sharply. Even if it were bluntly said that Jesus *became* God, we should not be greatly horrified; for (disregarding certain elegant refinements and even sublimities of expression) this is substantially what very many mean when they speak of the divinity of Jesus Christ. This is not really a paradoxical, nor even a difficult assertion, if we take no thought of the infinite qualitative difference and believe that every man is at least in some small part divine. It is not difficult to allow that Jesus was *more* divine than other men—perhaps than any other man. From this point of view Jesus is all the more precious to us as an *example*, for it is plain that what he *became* (starting without any advantage over us, unless it was a certain dose of religious genius) we also might become—if we cared to take the pains. If I dwell on this longer than may seem to you necessary, it is because Barth so much insists that this *hybris*—the pretense to be like God—was the first sin of man and the root of all sin.

The second way of dealing with the paradox takes it much more seriously. It recognizes more clearly than we commonly do the infinite qualitative difference between man and God, and it concedes that there is no way from man to God, but only from God to man. For the classical example of this way of solving the paradox we can refer to the early heresy of Docetism, which declined to think that the transcendent God had really become man, and represented instead that God took temporary abode in the man Jesus, from the time of his baptism until (and only until) he was nailed to the Cross. This is not essentially different from the Hindu notion of an *avatar*—except that it lasted longer, and that there was no visible demonstration of divine majesty and power. The Synoptic Gospels make it plain that Jesus did not account the miracles which he performed a proof of his messiahship (not to say a manifestation of divinity!) but only as signals which might well be heeded as a presage of the coming kingdom of God. Schweitzer remarks upon the astonishing fact that the Evangelists who knew so well the secret let it appear only occasionally. Barth insistently affirms that in Jesus God was strictly *"incognito"* (a word of Kierkegaard's); that God was not *manifested* in Jesus in the days of his flesh—*except* by the light of the Resurrection. How different is this from the idea of a theophany, in which it is supposed that God clearly makes himself known as God, appears and is seen as God, or at least as an angelic being producing a numinous effect. But all of these are old ideas. The modern unromantic equivalent is the idea that God imparted divinity to Jesus, infused into him divine quality. This, however, is not paradoxical, unless we could say it with a sense of the infinite qualitative difference between the divine and the human. But then *could* we say it any more easily than "God-Man?" At all events it is very far from saying that God became man—God the Son, the Second Person of the Trinity. For divine quality is not at all the same thing as divine personality—and even to say divine personality is not to say the same thing as God. We must remark by the way that the Church has never, in any considerate declaration or definition, been satisfied with saying that Jesus was *divine*.

There remains another way—and only one other way—of facing the paradox involved in the name Jesus Christ. This time really *facing* it, not venturing to "deal" with it, to mitigate it and resolve it, nor even to pry into the awe-inspiring secret it conceals. That is the dialectical way. The Calcedonian declaration unfalteringly faces the paradox, makes no attempt to disguise it, but is dialectical in every line: "The same complete in deity and complete in humanity, the same verily God and verily man, . . . of the same nature with the Father in respect to his deity and of the same nature with us in respect to his humanity, . . . made known in two natures, unmixed, unconfused, unseparated, undivided, the differences of the two natures not being confounded in the unity, but rather, with the peculiarities of each nature preserved, both united in one person and one mode of being." These words which have long been strange to us, which many have never heard, and do not like to hear even in the echo that reaches us through the so-called Athenasian Creed, I read to you because Barth prints them in Greek and follows them by saying, "That is the result which we also came to in our discussion above. If one desires to explain the fact of revelation in the terms which are necessary to thought, if he is willing thoughtfully to do justice to it, *this* is what he will be compelled to say, in the very same or in other words." And again later, "The purpose of this fundamental dogma of the Incarnation is today not less necessary than it then was." This of itself would almost suffice to give you an idea of Barth's Christology. For my part, I cannot wonder that so dialectical a man finds this very dialectical formula so congenial. But when I tell you that in this same chapter of his *Dogmatics* he argues for the necessity of the Virgin Birth of our Lord and justifies the title Mother of God as applied to Mary, some may be inclined to hear no more about the theology of Karl Barth.

You may wonder why it is that Barth, though by some he is reckoned as a prophet, is *not* reckoned among the orthodox and seeks no alliance with them. It is because he is consistently dialectical, is resolved to *stay* in a position which is not a "position" but a state of tension induced by the paradox; because he resists the pressure of traditional authority to adopt a given position, as well as the allurement of the reason to synthesize contradictions—"and then go on" triumphantly. Because he abides by the paradox he cannot regard truth (Christian truths among others) as a faith once for all delivered, as a "deposit" which can be simply handed on from one to another, relieving the individual of the need of seeking with fear and trembling, of putting his own anxious questions to God and hearing them returned to him as the answer, of the necessity of personal decision in the "existential Moment," of the deep disturbance at finding himself "contemporaneous" with Christ, of hearing God speak as "*this* God to *this* man," and of the requirement that faith must be faith (*i.e.* a tension between two poles, "a comforted despair," *desperatio fiducialis*) and not *assent*. A Chinese sage of the Zen school of Buddhism said to his monks, "The Doctrine is like a red hot lump of ice in the throat, which you cannot get up—and you cannot get down." Barth, I am sure, would not resent the application of this saying to the Christian Doctrine.

Here I quote to you a page of the *Dogmatics* (p. 257), which in detail is less paradoxical than most of Barth's pages, and yet shows how consistently he abides by the paradox. I select this page principally because it gives the context of a sentence quoted above, which taken alone might seem more reactionary than it is.

"Just as the doctrine of the Incarnation is only to be understood against the background of the Trinity, so this in turn can be understood only against that foreground. So then here (as in the case of the doctrine of the Trinity) there is evidently no desire to pry impertinently into a mystery so as to abolish the mysteriousness of it, but rather the will to face the fact upon which the Church is grounded and to which Christian preaching appeals, and to abide by it as an unfathomable secret worthy of all reverence, recognizing the necessity of knowing this mystery as a mystery and continuing to recognize it as such, the will, therefore, to define it precisely as a mystery and so to defend it against all importunate curiosity—that is what was aimed at in the theological construction which reached a climax in the formula of Calcedon which established the dialectical difference and unity of the divine and the human in Christ. Whether this effort to fix and define the mystery as a mystery is rightly to be regarded as so important and necessary, one can contest as against the early Church and its theology, only in case one is ready to contest that the church rightly conceived that it was dealing with an unfathomable mystery worthy of utmost reverence. If one does not contest this fact, then must the purpose of this second fundamental dogma, the dogma of the Incarnation, be understood as not less necessary today than it was then. This, however, is a fact which cannot be contested. In its essential significance Revelation is identical with Atonement. In the fact that the Word of God is uttered to man, it accomplishes in time the abolition of the antithesis between God and man, of the opposition in which man finds himself with respect to God and to himself. To say that God reveals himself, means that he reveals himself as the Redeemer who *atones*. He makes a man a question to himself, and he answers that question. Revelation is the act of God which relates to the Fall of man, to the perversion of the original relationship of man to him which was grounded in the Creation. In the unfaithfulness of man to him triumphs the faithfulness of God. Hence it is that it is a mystery, that in its *How?* it is incomprehensible. To the paradox of the Fall corresponds the fact that the Atonement can be made intelligible only as a paradox. It is not a matter of course, it is a miracle, it is *the* miracle which the Church contemplates as the fact upon which it is grounded—that in our unfaithfulness God's faithfulness triumphs, that God reveals himself, that the Word becomes flesh."

I turn to a different matter when I call your attention to the frequent assertion of Barth's that God is always *the subject*—never an object, never a predicate. This he insists upon chiefly with regard to revelation. *God* speaks, God reveals *himself*. No one can speak *about* God (as an object), unless it be God himself. This consideration is appropriate *here* as a warning against the common error of regarding Jesus Christ as *divine,* treating divinity (*i.e.* God) as an attribute, as a predicate of humanity. Which inevitably suggests that there might be a way from man to God. We conceive that we are expressing adequately the faith of the Church when (translating the oldest and most fundamental formula of the faith) we say: *Jesus Christ is Lord.* In fact that does say a great deal, if we understand what *Kyrios* meant in the syncretism of Greek and Oriental religion, and still more if we understand what it meant to the Jews, as the form in which the unpronounceable Name was pronounced, as *Jahve-Kyrios*. And yet we do *not* say what the early Church meant when we make Lord (*Kyrios*) a predicate of Jesus Christ. It is not merely a matter of curious philological interest to observe that in the solemn formula of the early Church[5] there was, in fact, no substantive (or should we call it copulative?) verb—and also that the title "Lord" does

---

[5] *Kyrios* Iesous Xristos, Phil. 2:11. Cf. Rom. 1:17. Common as is the order Kyrios X. I. (or I. X.), only once do we find X. I. Kyrios, namely in 2 Cor. 4:5, where we rightly translate, "proclaim J. C. *as* Lord." Christ Jesus occurs twice in the N. T.; Christ the Lord only in Luke 2:11, 26.

not stand at the end, in the position of a predicate, but emphatically at the beginning. *"Lord Jesus Christ"* is the concise and solemn form of this early confession of faith. This order of words was invariable, except where Jesus Christ is spoken of as *"our Lord."* *

These Scriptural considerations may help us to understand how much Barth means when he insists that God is never to be used as a predicate. This is the meaning of his contention (so hostile to our favorite opinion) that in the earthly life of Jesus, "the historical Jesus," God would not be discoverable—were it not that the incognito was discarded by the resurrection of Jesus from the dead. That is evidently what Paul meant to say when, in a sentence which was an offense to the generation in which many of us were born, he expressed his comparative indifference to "Christ according to the flesh." If we had only Christ according to the flesh, he would say, and if Christ be not raised from the dead, "we are of all men most pitiable." Our preaching is vain, your faith is vain, we are convicted of being false witnesses of God—and we are yet in our sins. "But in fact Christ hath been raised from the dead"—therefore *everything* is different, and also "the days of his flesh" are seen in a new light. Decidedly, Barth does not seek to found the Christian faith upon the "historical

---

* It was a matter of course that in the "apology" for Christianity the assertion was constantly made that Jesus *is* the Christ; but *in* the Church this great assertion was simply assumed in the Name *Jesus-Christ*. Also it was a matter of course that in the Gospels, seeing that their theme is the story of the earthly life, the human name *Jesus* predominates, and the title *Christ*, where it is used, follows it as a predicate. It is remarkable that this use did not persist unchanged, and that in the Epistles Christ Jesus is used alternatively with it. In the Epistles there is only one place where the name Jesus is used alone as it was in the Gospels. That is 2 Cor. 4:10, where the reason is obvious.

Jesus"—nor yet, apart from it, upon the mythical idea of a Christ.

Here is a place where I quote Barth again—this time it is his comment on Rom. 1:4, which he translates thus: "Mightily constituted as Son of God according to the Holy Ghost by his resurrection from the dead."

"This 'constitution' is the true significance of Jesus —which, to be sure, is a thing which obviously cannot be historically determined. Jesus as the *Christ,* the Messiah, is the End of time, and is only to be understood as Paradox (Kierkegaard), only as Victor (Blumhardt), only as Pre-history (Overbeck). Jesus as the Christ is the plane totally unknown to us which intersects our plane perpendicularly from above. Jesus as the Christ can, within the plane of historical visibility, be understood *only* as problem, *only* as myth. Jesus as the Christ brings here the world of the Father, of which we in the plane of historical visibility know nothing and can know nothing.—But the Resurrection of the dead is the turning point, the conjunction of that line which descends from above with the corresponding perception from below. The Resurrection is the *revelation,* the discovery of Jesus as the Christ, the manifestation of God and the recognition of God in him, the entrance of the necessity of giving God the glory and of reckoning with the unknown and the invisible factors in Jesus Christ, letting him count as the End of time, as the Paradox, as Pre-history. In the Resurrection the new world of the Holy Ghost touches the old world of flesh. But touches it, like the tangent to a circle, without touching it; and precisely because it does *not* touch it, it touches it as its limit, as the *new* world. So the resurrection was in a sense that event outside the gates of Jerusalem in the year 30, inasmuch as it there actually occurred and was discerned and recognized. But on the other hand it was not that at all, inasmuch as its necessity, manifestation and revelation, so far from being conditioned by that occurring and discerning and recognizing, was itself the condition of all this. Inasmuch as Jesus reveals himself and is discovered as the Messiah, he is already *before* Easter Day "constituted as Son of God," just as certainly as he was *after* Easter.—That is the significance of Jesus: the constitution of the Son of Man as *Son of God*. What apart from this he is, is just as important and just as unimportant as everything temporal, material and human can be in itself. 'If we have known Christ after the flesh, so know we him now no more.' In that he *was*, he *is;* and in that he *is*, what he *was* lies behind. Here no espousal, no amalgamation, takes place between God and men, no soaring of men up to God, or pouring out of God into human nature; but what touches us in Jesus the Christ, in that it does not touch us, is the kingdom of God, the Creator and Redeemer. It has become actual, it has come near (3:21 f.)."

In the *Dogmatics* this "miracle perpendicular from above" is spoken about in calmer language, but not discounted, not explained, and not explained away. There, too, the historical Jesus is the point where eternity touches time tangentially; but the significance of that point can be apprehended only by discerning whence that tangential line came and whither it goes. For this reason Barth dwells predominantly upon the Source, which is beyond the birth; and upon the End, the Resurrection, which is beyond the death—both of them then entirely beyond history. Barth would be the last to deny that this miracle defies the impossibility of bridging the distance which divides time and eternity. He would say that only God can defy it, God alone. There *is* a way from God to man.

Death and resurrection are two themes which are always prominent in Barth's thought. It goes without saying that his thoughts on these two great subjects are summed up in his comment on 1 Cor. 15, a book which he entitles *The Resurrection of the Dead*. This preoccupation with death is a trait which in large part determines the character of his theology. If he had thought as constantly of life, and of man's ardent thirst for life which gives death its terrible significance, he would have been closer to Unamuno, who shows in his book *The Tragic Sense of Life*[7] that he too is a disciple of Kierkegaard, but a Catholic disciple. However, the stress upon *agony* and the *tragic* sense of life shows that we have here only a difference of emphasis.

In dealing with this topic it would not be possible to conceal, even if one would, the strident conflict between Barth's doctrine and . . . if I may not say *ours*, I will say, the doctrines which most commonly prevail among us. It may be that the Theology of Crisis will be all the more resolutely repudiated in America the better it is known—and chiefly for the reason that it has decisively rejected the notion that the Christian faith can be founded upon the historical Jesus. And yet, perhaps, more persons than we imagine have already become disquieted by the reflection that, starting with the historical Jesus alone, we cannot by any conceivable stretch of the imagination get higher than the idea of a man whose predicate is God.

Only the colder scholars operate with the conception of "the historical Jesus," while preachers use a word of far more pathos, "the humanity of Christ." The enthusiasm of their preaching is supported, and

---

[7] In other works, too, and particularly in *L'Agonie du Christianisme*, which he wrote while he was an exile in France.

the ardent response of the people is stimulated, by the proud consciousness that now for the first time in history we have discovered that Jesus was really and truly a man. The conviction that historical reality is on their side makes them bold to ridicule, attack and destroy the old dogma of the Person of Christ.

Whether they have reality on their side depends upon the question, whether what they call "humanity" does in fact describe what humanity is. The humanistic idea of humanity was derived, it is clear, from the Renascence, and that in turn was dependent upon the classical age of Roman literature. But not many reflect how extraordinary an age *that* was. Unamuno says of it (citing Flaubert) that it was the only period in history when men could enjoy the pround consciousness of being supreme in the universe, as the only exponents of its indwelling reason, without any Gods above them—and, we may add, without our disturbing knowledge of kinship with the beasts below us. Characteristic was Cicero's dictum that, even if there were Gods, it were better not to risk any dealings with them. When humanism was revived again in the Renascence, at a time when few doubted that there was a God, it was a foregone conclusion that the idea of deity would not be allowed to disturb the superb conception which had been formed of man, but rather would be used to exalt it. This could be accomplished by the notion of the immanence of the divine in man. In fact, that conception has become so common that man does not seem to us fully described when he is described merely as body, soul and spirit, without any reference to the "divine spark."

Such a conception of human nature not only makes the old Christological dogma seem absurd, but it disposes easily of the question which was debated by the early Church with so much concern and answered so dialectically. The question how a divine and a human nature could be united in Jesus Christ is no longer a serious question when it is recognized that all men are in a measure divine and therefore are in some degree already united with God. What distinguishes Jesus from other men is only the degree and intensity of this union. Consequently, the old problem of Christology is replaced by discussion about the God-ward-consciousness of Jesus, and the question how others can in a measure partake of it.

But again (and this time more seriously) we must raise the question whether the humanistic conception of humanity corresponds with what man really is. The lineage of this conception as I have traced it would not suffice to discredit it if it is true. But it may suggest that it may need to be put to the test in our day. The real test is whether it proves to be a true picture of man as we know him—by introspection, candid and deep, and by circumspection, critical but friendly. What about man as we learn to know him through the newspapers, which we sadly regard as a transcript of life? Or in politics, in business, in the trades, in the rackets, in the Church, in the school and in the family? Our judgment of man may remain doubtful, in spite of all this. But *at least* doubtful! It is not reasonable that in theology we should hold firmly to the most exalted idea of man, when at the same time we are depressed by the altogether sordid account of man which we read in so many books, or by the tragic protest of Nietzsche that "man is a thing which must be surpassed!" or by the comforted despair of Dostoiewski, who sees so much good in the worst, but so much bad in the best, and shudderingly detects at last, in place of the divinity we boast of, the power of darkness, a daemonia, which proudly asserts, "I am Satan, nothing that is human is alien to me"—and with that destroys for us the favorite text of humanism! And are we not compelled to take note of the conflict which modern theology has provoked at this point between science and religion? For the "deep" psychology of Freud, Jung and Adler, the deeper it delves in the human heart, the less it discovers of the divinity which we assume to be there. Instead of that it discovers an all-devastating *libido*, or a no less devastating *ego* with its presumption of "God-almightiness." In reading these psychologists I am reminded of a patient of Elwood Worcester's who exclaimed, "How many windows the soul has which look out straight upon hell!" The superficial psychology of Behaviorism gives us no more comfort—if indeed it allows us still to conceive that there is a soul in which divinity might dwell. How can we forget that the human nature (our nature!) which Christ took upon him was, as he conceived of it and as he experienced it, subject to Satan—with the possibility of subjecting itself to God? In any case *subject!* If we think in that way of the humanity of Christ, we are aware of a deeper pathos than Liberal Theology discovers. For we have been taught of late to think of Christ as assuming an *ideal* humanity. We suppose that this is meant by the Scripture when it says he was without sin. Consequently it does not seem to us a humiliation for God to become man. We cannot understand why in the Creed men should feel constrained to bend the knee in amazed reverence at the humility of God, not at the place which laconically describes the last abasement ("suffered under Pontius Pilate, crucified, dead and buried"), but at the simple affirmation, "and was made man." The "distance" between God and man does not impress us as great. These other distances we have familiar standards for measuring, and they seem vast to us. The distance between a man of means and honorable station—and a servant! Between a reputable servant—and a wretch who is condemned as a criminal and nailed to a cross! That distance is immense, but the distance between the divine and the divinely human seems hardly so great to us.

But for the early Church the pathos of this distance was most real. And it must be conceded at least that the opinion which the Church expressed about humanity is not different from that which is everywhere reflected in the Bible. Up to this point I have been following freely a late article by Gogarten.[8] I proceed now to quote literally. "It requires no great perspicacity to see that the Biblical conception of men, and hence of the relationship between God and man, is fundamentally different from the modern conception. In the first place, immanence is not to be found in the Bible. The God of the Bible is distinctly not 'something divine' which a man might carry within him or which in any way whatever could belong to his nature. It is true that in the view of the Bible, both the Old and the New Testament, God and man belong most closely together. But they do not belong in one another. They belong together like master and servant, father and son. But just in this way they belong together and not otherwise. . . . Precisely the closeness of the relationship which exists between God and man, as the Bible understands it, makes an immanence of the divine in the human impossible. This closeness of relationship, this sense of belonging together, is a strictly personal relationship between God and man. It consists in the fealty of man to God. Here immanence makes no sense.

Man's fealty can be considered in the aspect of

---

[8] *Menchheit und Gottheit Jesu Christi*, in *Zwischen den Zeiten*, Heft 1, for 1932.

obedience or in the aspect of disobedience. When we speak of men in connection with the Redeemer it is disobedient men we have in mind. The disobedient man is characterized as under the Law. For the disobedient man is not by his disobedience freed from the obligations of fealty, but he is under the Law. That Law which, whatever he may make of it, tells him that he has resisted God and is and remains a rebel against God. Hence, because the Law is connected with disobedience and resistance to God—law is only where disobedience is—therefore is the curse associated with the Law. This is the curse which rests upon him who does not fulfill the Law. He however who has come to this pass of being under the law, that is, who once has fallen from God, cannot fulfill the Law. He can indeed *do* what the Law requires, but he can in no case *be* what the Law requires. Or, to use St. Paul's language, man can at the most attain to willing what the Law proposes, but not to the doing of it (Rom. 7:11 ff). Man cannot possibly be righteous before God through the Law, as the Jews and all who trust in the Law are inclined to imagine. Hence the curse which rests upon disobedience is inseparably bound up with the Law. And the curse of the Law means the reign of sin and of death over men. Hence this being-bound-under-the-Law-and-its-curse is what constitutes human nature. And only one who takes this into account understands man as the Bible understands him. Now precisely of this human nature it is declared that the Logos, God's Son, took it upon him. That the Logos became flesh—that means above everything else that he who is God is subjected to the Law and its curse, having subjected himself to it. *This,* above everything else, must be said, if we are really to speak of the humanity of Jesus Christ. Everything else which can and must be said needs to be said from this standpoint—as *e.g.* that Christ shared the physical and historical limitations natural to man."

That this is Biblical doctrine you hardly need quotations to remind you—as this from St. Paul, "Him who knew no sin he made sin for us" (2 Cor. 5:21), and "having become a curse for us" (Gal. 3:13); and from the Epistle to the Hebrews, "who was tempted like as we are" and "learned obedience through suffering." What I would remark upon is, that contrasting these hard sayings with the very easy ones of modern theology we can hardly feel that the humanity of Christ was only lately discovered and its deepest pathos divined.

I have already told you nearly as much about the Barthian conception of the Person of Christ as the space at my disposal permits. You may be disappointed to see that substantially there is nothing new in it. In fact, it is expressly the old doctrine. It must be evident that a theology of crisis could be satisfied with nothing *less* than this. For where would the *crisis* be if Christ challenged us merely as a man and not as God, if the Gospel were not a voice out of eternity but merely a relatively comforting and relatively disquieting voice out of time itself.

> All this took place, you think,
> Only to give our joys a zest
> And prove our sorrows for the best?

And as a dialectical theology it could not propose anything *more* than the old dialectical dogma—any solution that would mitigate the paradox, or any synthesis that would resolve it. The name Jesus Christ would not remain dialectical, if it were not respected as a paradox—which must be believed because it is incredible. It must be evident also that it is alto-

THE MEDIATOR

gether undialectical to regard the Messiahship of Jesus as a question which can be dealt with and determined like an historical fact.

If there is anything peculiar in the Dialectical Theology at this point, it is the inclination to regard Christ predominantly as the Mediator. *Der Mittler* is the title of one of Brunner's more important books. This must necessarily be a favorite title for all who have a sense of the "distance" between God and man. In fact, the sense of "distance" is hardly ever lacking in unsophisticated men, and wherever it has been clearly felt men have recognized the need of a mediator. Where it has been felt as absolute there has never been any doubt that the Mediator must be God and not man. No Prometheus has ever figured as Mediator. The Prophets—however extravagant it may seem!—were forced to conclude that the Mediator must be Immanuel, God-with-us. There is no reason to feel embarrassment at the necessity of admitting that the sense of need prompted a conception of Christ (the "preëxistent Jesus"?) *before* the Advent—and also *after* it, and in places remote from the tradition of Israel. What may be called the evangelical development of Buddhism in China and Japan invented the gracious figure of Kuan-yin. I feel no difficulty in conceding that this figure points *back* to Jesus as decisively as the Prophets pointed *forward*. And if there were *now* no such need felt, there would assuredly be no faith in Christ. The figure of Kuan-yin is as clearly and definitely celestial as was the prophetic conception of "one like unto a son of man." It was also as definitely anthropomorphic, for it was an expression of "Mercy, Pity, Peace and Love."

> For Mercy has a human heart;
> Pity, a human face;
> And Love, the human form divine;
> And Peace the human dress.

And yet *not* human, for Kuan-yin is neither clearly man nor clearly woman. But chiefly is it not human because

> Cruelty has a human heart,
>   And Jealousy a human face:
> Terror the human form divine,
>   And Secrecy the human dress.
>
> The human dress is forgèd iron,
>   The human form a fiery forge,
> The human face a furnace sealed,
>   The human heart its hungry gorge.

William Blake significantly puts these *last* lines among the "Songs of Experience."

As Mediator, Christ was expected to *do* something—and Jesus did it. Kuan-yin and other mythical Christs did nothing, and could do nothing to produce a real effect in the past, because they were not historical. They cannot even be *conceived* as doing anything except with relation to the future, as a promise to help. But this is not the place to consider that topic, which must be left to the seventh lecture.

Apart from what he did, there is immense importance in what Christ *is* as Mediator. It is characteristic of the Barthian Theology that it thinks predominately of the Mediator as Revealer. But Revelation is the topic of the next lecture. I need say here only, by way of anticipation, that revelation is to be regarded also as an act, as a deed.

LECTURE VI

REVELATION

Revelation (or the Word of God, as Barth and Brunner prefer to say) is a theme more insisted upon than any other by the School of Crisis; not because it is substantially the most important theme, but because it is evidently the *first* question to be faced by a theology which declares at the outset that our God is the unknown God. Theology must stop abruptly with that initial assertion—unless the miracle happens that God speaks and reveals *himself*. For there is no way from man to God, but only from God to man. We have become familiar with the principles which determine in detail the character of the Theology of Crisis. The recognition of the infinite qualitative difference between time and eternity, and therefore of the "distance" between man and God, though it furnishes no answer to the question whether in fact God has spoken, makes it obviously necessary that God should speak, if we are to know anything about him. "With God all things are possible," and we have no reasonable ground for denying that, in spite of the "distance," there is a way from God to man; but whether God in his sovereign freedom has been pleased to use that way cannot be determined by any principle. It is a question of fact. Or rather, as all the theologians of this school would agree in saying, it is a question of *actuality*. Properly understood, the difference between these two terms is momentous. For a question of fact is always a question about the past, even if it be a past which endures up to the present; whereas the word actual indicates decisively the *present moment* in which an act occurs, abstracting attention from the past and from the future. When we *reflect* upon any occurrence in time we are compelled to regard it as a link in the chain of cause and effect, having its cause in the past and its effects in the future. Nevertheless, at the moment of experiencing it we are not necessarily aware of this. We may be absorbed in the occurrence itself as actual. And when God speaks we must understand *this* occurrence simply as actual. Though his having spoken may conceivably have consequences for the future, it cannot be traced to any cause or causes in the past. For according to the principles we have in mind, God's word, if it comes at all, can come only from outside the temporal order, *i.e.* from eternity, like a line falling perpendicularly from above. When we say that revelation is a question not of fact but of actuality we completely alter the statement of the problem as it was conceived by Protestant as well as by Catholic orthodoxy. The question now is not first of all whether God *spoke*—some time in the past, more or less remote—and by what criterion we can determine that the record of this speech, a word recorded in Holy Scripture, was really a Word of God. Instead, it is a question whether God actually speaks, now, at this moment and to *me*. And whether I *hear*. For *if* I hear a word addressed to me in God's voice, the question cannot arise *how* I am to recognize it as God's Word. And if I do not thus hear it, I can have no interest in asking such a question. The doctrine of the Reformers that the Word of God authenticates itself, or is authenticated to the individual by the testimony of the Holy Ghost, is much more evidently applicable here than in the connection in which they used it. Regarded as *actual*, the Word of God is either heard as the Word of God, or it is not heard at all. If it is heard, it puts us under the necessity of answering. There are only two possible answers, Yes and No. Yes, is the answer of faith; and faith is no more than Yes.

It may be objected that this makes faith no more than bare "assent"—and we know how little *that* means in the Roman doctrine! But observe that here we are not talking about belief in a proposition, a formal expression of a general truth which can be communicated by one man to another, and to which, perhaps, we can the more easily assent because we do not understand it; but we are talking about assent to God's Word addressed directly to us, which always is a command, and always is intelligible in so far as we hear it at all. Faith is therefore much more than such assent as might be required of one who is in the aloof position of an observer. For *this* is the sure criterion of a Word of God, that it cannot come to us at all without wrenching us out of the secure and detached position of an observer and throwing us into crisis, into the absolute Crisis, which demands the absolute Decision, Either-Or and All or Nothing. The Word of God coming to us constitutes the Moment, and it does not come to us at all except as it comes to us individually. Here, Yes and No mean infinitely more than assent and dissent. For Yes means obedience; and No, disobedience. Faith is simply Yes, *i.e.* simply obedience—it is all of that . . . and no more. "We are unprofitable servants," we have merely *heard* God's Word—and have *not* disobeyed it. Barth describes faith as "mere emptiness" (*Hohlraum*). If that seem an extravagant expression, you will at least not fail to recognize that there is excuse for it as a protest against our tendency to attribute the utmost *fulness* to faith. We can hardly manage *not* to regard it as meritorious. For regarding it positively and as a religious act, it has evidently more value than anything else that we do— more than any *good work*—because it reveals more clearly what we *are,* namely, religious men, with a zeal for God, and with a temperament and disposition to respond to the numinous with appropriate feeling and imagination—in short, with all the fulness of fantasy and emotion which our mystical endowment may render us capable of. It is clear that the Theology of Crisis relegates faith to a more humble rôle. And yet it ascribes to it a decisive rôle when it regards it as the absolute Decision in response to God's Word. It regards it, moreover, as the possibility of every man, irrespective of the question whether he is distinguished or not by the possession of a religious or mystical disposition.

I have been speaking about the general principles which determine the point of view from which the Theology of Crisis *must* regard the question of revelation. You will not have failed to observe that here we are dealing again with the key words of Kierkegaard, and especially with the two categories he most emphasizes: Contemporaneousness and the Individual. The Moment of Decision which he makes so much of is determined by the contemporaneousness of God and Christ. Hence it is that the Moment is not simply a moment of time, but a moment lifted out of time by the fact that God speaks—*this* God to *this* man, here and now. It is no longer merely time, but "the acceptable time," a moment qualified by eternity, the "existential Moment," in which a man, by his Decision to answer God by a Yes, becomes what he *is.*

These categories are essential to the understanding

of revelation as the Critical Theology conceives it; and in order to fix your attention upon them I quote from Kierkegaard a passage which, though it may seem long, is in fact very much abbreviated.[1] Kierkegaard is commenting here upon James 1:25-27. The subject of the whole section is: "What is requisite in order to behold one's self in the mirror of the Word with real edification?" He begins with the thesis: "First of all it is requisite that you do not look at the mirror, so as to behold the mirror, but that you behold yourself in the mirror." Ten pages of ironical comment are devoted to the exposure of the fallacy that the "objective" study of the Bible, as recommended by scholars to the vulgar, can avail for edification. Then comes the positive thesis which more properly concerns us here: "When you read God's Word in order to behold yourself in the mirror (if really you would behold yourself) you must say to yourself constantly, 'It is I that am here spoken to, it is about me all this is said.'"

"Do not let yourself be duped—and do not deceive yourself. For unfortunately we men are very cunning in dealing with God and his Word. Even the stupidest of us is so cunning. Yes, flesh and blood and self-love are very cunning. So it occurs to us to say (though naturally we do not admit that we are moved thereto by the desire to protect ourselves against God and his Word—we are not stupid enough for that, for that would deprive us of the profit of our sly invention)— we light, I say, upon the clever thought, that to think about ourselves (so we slyly put it!) would be vanity, morbid vanity. (That may indeed in certain situations be the case, but not precisely then when we ought to let God's Word have dominion over us!) 'Fye for

---

Zur Selbstprufung der Gegenwart anbefohlen, pp. 18-36.

shame at the notion of being so vain! For to think about one's self and to say, That is I, would be what the learned call subjectivity, and subjectivity is vanity. The vanity of supposing that I can read no book (God's Word!) without conceiving that it refers to me—must I not abhor it? And could I be stupid enough not to, considering that this is the way to ensure myself against the danger that God's Word might actually get a grip on me? Should I not, therefore, instead of allowing my vanity to bring me into a personal (subjective) relation to the Word, rather, with the true seriousness which is so highly praised by the world, transform it into an impersonal something, to which I could then (how serious and cultured!) comport myself objectively, free from all vulgar vanity which would prompt me to intrude my own personality and suppose that this is all about me, always about me? No, far be from me such vulgar vanity! And far be it from me, too, that the Word (a thing which could so easily occur) might find me, me individually, and gain the mastery over me! So that I might not be any longer able to ward it off, so that it would persecute me then till it drove me to the obedient renunciation of this world, or at least to the honest confession that I do not renounce it—and so I would suffer well deserved punishment for the fact that I had treated God's word in such a vulgar way!'

"No, no, no! At every reading of the divine Word, to say to yourself constantly, 'This is said about me and to me," that is what it is to be serious, precisely that is seriousness.—Hence that is what everyone who has had the highest interests of Christianity at heart has again and again insisted upon as the decisive thing, the unconditional condition of attaining the end of seeing one's self in the mirror.

That therefore is what you must do. You must say to yourself constantly as you read, 'This is spoken to me, this is said about me.' "

Then after commenting at length upon various places where the Word of God was personally applied, and especially upon Nathan's application of his parable to David, he comes to the story of the good Samaritain.

" 'There was a man who went from Jerusalem to Jericho and fell among thieves, who stripped him of his raiment and wounded him, leaving him half dead.' When you read further, 'And by chance there came down a certain priest that way, and when he saw him he passed by on the other side'—then you must say, 'this is I.' You must not try to prove an alibi, least of all by a witticism (for though in the worldly world a witticism may serve to get a man out of the most humiliating position, it does not serve so well when you are reading the Word of God); you must not say, 'This was a priest, and I am no priest; and it is a good thing that the Gospel puts priests in this damaging light, for they really are a bad lot.' No, when you read God's Word you must be serious and say to yourself, 'I am this priest. Oh, that ever I could show myself so unmerciful, I who call myself a Christian and as such am a priest (an argument we very well know how to urge when we wish to make ourself independent of priests and proclaim the priesthood of all believers). Oh, that I could be so unmerciful, that I could actually see this without being moved to sympathy—and I actually saw it, as the Gospel says, "and he saw him, and passed by on the other side." '—'And likewise a levite, when he was at the place, came and looked on him, and passed by on the other side.' Here you must say, 'This is I. Oh, that I could be so hard hearted, and for a second time! not being bettered by my former experience!'—And a certain practical man as he journed came where he was and said to himself, 'What is this? Here is a man half dead. There can be no profit in going over there; it might involve me in a law suit, or the police might come along this minute and suspect me of the crime.' There you must say to yourself, 'This is I. Oh, that I could be so miserably shrewd—and still worse! that I could tell this story to an acquaintance and accept his praise for my practical good sense!'—Then there came that way another man in such deep thought he was not thinking at all. He saw nothing and went by. There you must say to yourself, 'That was I. What a blockhead! that I could pass that spot and not notice that a man was lying there half dead!' That at least is what you would say to yourself if a precious treasure were lying on the road and you happened to pass by without noticing it.—'But a certain Samaritain as he journed came where he was'—you know the rest. And here, since you are wearied of the perpetual 'This is I,' you can say for a change, 'This is not I. Unfortunately, this is not like me.' When at the conclusion of the parable Jesus says to the Pharisee, 'Go and do thou likewise,' you are to say to yourself, 'That applies to me—up then and doing!' You must not try to side-step, least of all by a witticism, which in a religious sense certainly does not better your situation, but only increases your condemnation. You must not say, 'I protest on my word of honor, I never saw a man half dead lying by the roadside who had fallen among robbers. Robbers are very rare in our parts anyway.' No, that is not the way you must speak. You must say, 'That word, "Go and do likewise," finds me.' For you understand the saying perfectly well. And if on a journey you have never encountered a man who was despoiled by robbers, there are wretched people enough along your path and mine. . . .

"These examples suffice to show how you should read God's Word. As superstition seeks to summon spirits by the recitation of incantations, so must you (that is the first need) by dint of continually reading God's Word in the manner I have indicated, read before long into your very soul such fear and trembling that by God's help you may be fortunate enough to become a man, a personality, and no longer an impersonal, objective thing, that terrible unreality to which men—made in God's image!—are so shamefully reduced."

Perhaps I have quoted more than enough to fix your attention upon the categories of Contemporaneousness and the Individual. In one place I used the phrase "finds me" to render an expression of Kierkegaard's. I used that phrase for the purpose of reminding you that the categories we are here dealing with are not strange to our English theological tradition. When we were first wrestling with the problem how to discover the Word within the Word, the word of revelation within the Bible, Coleridge gave us the clue, by his once famous expression, "This word finds me." Coleridge, you may remember, was accounted the father of English theological liberalism, before it had suffered the German transformation and became the Liberal Theology which we now know. The second aphorism in his *Aids to Reflection* is: "There is one sure way of giving freshness and importance to the most common-place maxims—that of reflecting upon them in direct reference to our own state and conduct, to our own past and future being." In a later part of the book he applies this to the reading of the Holy Scripture. This apprehension, so calmly and judiciously expressed by Coleridge, needs only to be radicalized (as the Germans say) in order to be an apt expression of the principle insisted upon by Kierkegaard and the Theology of Crisis.

Before going further I must remark that the topic of revelation, though it is the topic we most need to hear discussed, and on which, perhaps, we would most earnestly seek enlightenment, is precisely the spot where Barth satisfies the fewest of us. It goes without saying that the Fundamentalists must be dissatisfied with a discussion of revelation which makes no account of "inspiration" and entirely rejects the notion of inerrancy. In this connection it is sufficient to cite the last paragraph of Bultmann's *The Idea of Revelation in the New Testament*.[1]

"But the demand that we say unequivocally which precisely is the Word of God must be rejected, because it rests upon the conception that is possible to indicate a collection of sentences which exist objectively and are to be objectively understood. What 'word of God' means can indeed be formally explained; but it is precisely this formal explanation which makes it clear that a 'content' of God's Word cannot be delivered like a manufactured article, but can only be had as it is heard time and again."

But also the Liberals will not be satisfied with the Barthian notion of revelation, for in this place, as in so many others, the Critical Theology is a polemic against Liberalism.

Finally, I am not disposed to deny that Barth fails here to satisfy even the serious and open minded enquirer. It is unfortunate that the one work of his which is available in English, suggests by its English title, *The Word of God*, that it will furnish a clear and systematic answer to our anxious enquiries about the meaning of revelation, and proves instead to be a

---
[1] *Der Begriff der Offenbarung im NT*, 1929.

THE DOCTRINE   163

collection of essays on *other* subjects, which justify the title only by the fact that Barth's favorite theme frequently emerges: "God speaks." We must suppose that in the 400 pages of the Prolegomena to his *Dogmatics* Barth has said all that he proposes to say on this subject, for this volume is entitled *The Doctrine of God's Word*. And yet it does not answer some of the questions we are most interested in putting to him. I find more passages in Brunner which can be quoted here with effect, and at the conclusion of this lecture I shall give an account of Bultmann's conception of revelation.

But there is one section of the *Dogmatics* (§ 4), entitled *Three Aspects of the Word of God*, which we can profitably consider at this point, and we are now in a position to understand it. The three aspects of the Word of God which Barth distinguishes are: Revelation, the Scriptures, and the Sermon. They are listed in this order, because this is the order of eminence. Revelation means a Word of God directly and personally imparted to a man. Holy Scripture is (among other things) a record of such words. It is to be remarked that "canonicity" is the only category Barth uses to define Scripture. He mentions the negative implication of canonicity: "Out of the din of apochryphal and heretical voices, these and only these voices are singled out as genuine Prophetic and Apostolic witnesses, with their historical and categorical imperative: Go ye and preach." But he emphasizes rather the positive aspect, "which was also primary in the notion of canonicity: the fact that such an historical and categorical imperative does indeed resound in the Scriptures." And he refers to the first years of the Reformation as an example of the significance of canonicity ("without or at least before the development of a doctrine of inspiration"); to "the enigmatical dynamic with which this old book, the Bible as such and as a whole, asserted for itself attention, respect and obedience, with the most revolutionary consequences for doctrine and life; to the amazing quantity and intensity of the *preaching* which issued from this historical factor, that is, from a glance into this book, as though it was being preached for the first time." You see from this what is meant by listing preaching as the third aspect of the Word. Preaching, as an office in the Church, depends upon the Scripture. It properly appeals to it for authority. For the Scripture, as the record of the Word of God, is always at hand objectively as the permanent possibility of a subjective crisis. It is the business of preaching to make it contemporary. And without putting himself above the Scripture or freeing himself from it, it is the duty of the preacher to "speak as it were oracles of God," to utter the Word of God as it has found him, with the same originality and intensity as if it had never been uttered before. Thus in the end, Barth recognizes that the three aspects unite in one. The word may spring from the printed page and claim a man as directly as the original revelation. Between these three aspects there is no absolute difference, though it is important to keep our categories clear and remember that "revelation is revelation, Scripture is Scripture, and preaching is preaching."

But what most challenges our attention here is the fact that when Barth comes to discuss in detail these three aspects he puts the last first, considering first of all the Word as it is preached. We are in a position to understand in what interest he does this. For the important thing is that God speaks. That he actually speaks no man can know but the man to whom he speaks, who recognizes God's voice by faith. Only such a man will be able to believe that God speaks also to other men and has so spoken in time past. By faith he will recognize God's Word also in the Scripture, and will be able to understand how the written Word (in spite of its imperfections) derives from an original revelation. Barth here is placing the emphasis where he always puts it, upon preaching as the medium through which God speaks, though doubtless it is not the only medium. With this understanding we may find Barth's frequent references to the Word of God more intelligible than they seemed to us before. And we may be grateful to him for indicating to us so clearly the point at which we must begin, if we are ever to come to an apprehension of the meaning and the reality of revelation.

But before we consider further what the Theology of Crisis is aiming at, we must go back and consider what it is aimed against, what is the meaning of the polemic involved in the discussion of this subject of revelation.

First of all it may be regarded as a polemic against the prevailing indifference to the problem of revelation. It is ominous to observe the fact that revelation is a word hardly ever used any more by our preachers or by their people. And though theologians find themselves bound to deal with it because it denominates an outstanding feature of the Christian tradition, they commonly are intent upon deforming the conception. It obviously is not a negligible feature of Christianity; and it is by no means invalidated (quite the contrary!) by the remark that this conception was inherited by Christianity from Judaism, whence Mohammed also inherited it. In fact, it is an idea prominent in many religions. I say therefore that it is ominous to observe that a word so important and so characteristic has been discarded from our speech —I do not say deliberately and resolutely discarded, but simply forgotten. It is not difficult to guess the cause of this neglect, if we note what word it is that is used in place of revelation, and in place also of faith, which is the counterpart of revelation. The word we use is *religion.* That is now a word which has become so indispensible to us whenever we would speak about Christianity that we can hardly credit the fact that the Bible gets along without using it—or, to speak more precisely, never uses it except with an implication of disparagement. And no wonder it is indispensible to us, since it takes the place both of revelation and of faith, and of all the great words which are associated with these terms. We say simply "religion" where the Bible speaks of God's acts, of God's revelations (his Word in time past and his Word now), and also where it speaks of man's response: the fear of God, faith and obedience. But when we say "religion" we do not say the same thing that the Bible says when it speaks of God's Word to man and of man's faith and obedience. It is clear, at all events, that religion does not always mean faith in Christ. Notoriously, there are many religions. And perhaps it has not escaped your attention that even in Christendom religion may mean disobedience, that it may mean to "leave the commandment of God and hold fast the traditions of men." The fact is, we have discarded the word revelation, not chiefly because it denotes an incredible conception (as indeed it does!), but because such a conception is superfluous so long as we are unaware of the "distance" between God and man. Religion is a conception which implies no real "distance," no qualitative difference between God and man. If there is any crisis involved in it, it is not the radical crisis effected by a challenge out of eternity. Our own heart asks all questions—and answers them. We challenge ourselves with the religion that is within us. That may produce a crisis and a conversion which involves even "the revaluation of all values," only it does not put *us* in crisis, our whole existence, as a challenge from out of eternity must do.

You can perceive here the meaning and the pathos of Barth's insistence upon the necessity of "reinstating the distance." Perhaps now you may not be inclined to find fault with him if you detect some exaggeration in that word. For if the distance is reinstated, we shall no longer be at a loss to appreciate the meaning and the necessity of revelation. We shall enquire only whether it is possible, and we shall ask that question earnestly. We shall understand also why the polemic is so sharply pointed against Schleiermacher's theology of experience and against distincter forms of mysticism. This is primarily a polemic against theologians, but it is waged for the sake of the *people,* who have been thoroughly though unconsciously infected by the theologians—even (or I might say, most of all) when they were scornful of theology.

If the "distance" is known to be real, and attempts to bridge it by feeling (*i.e.* "Christian experience" and mysticism) are shown to be delusions, inasmuch as feeling and experience lie wholly on *this* side of the hair line between time and eternity, and do not really pass it; then there remains only the possibility that this distance may be traversed by the Word, the intelligent and intelligible Logos. We may reasonably think here of *our* word uttered in prayer. But how much more weighty and important is God's Word to us! This undoubtedly is the possibility contemplated in the Bible—and not only contemplated as a possibility, but asserted as a reality and abundantly exemplified by instances of man's speech to God and of God's speech to man. The Bible is the record of a colloquy between man and God. And it is important to observe that God speaks first, and that he speaks even in man's question. It is the apprehension of this fact which is expressed by Pascal: "Thou wouldest not be seeking me, had I not found thee." Adam did not first ask, "O God, where art thou?" nor even ask, "Where am I?" until God asked, "Where art thou Adam?" Not till God asks me, "Where art thou?" do I come to myself. This means that the Word of God, if it is really God's Word, is not our discovery but is in the strictest sense a revelation. Also, if it is really God's Word, nothing could be more impertinent than to enquire about its "value," as a Pragmatist would do, when our whole attention should be fixed anxiously upon its *meaning*.

I quote from Brunner.[a] "Man's freedom and spirituality is grounded entirely and only upon his power to hear and understand, upon the fact that he can hear and understand the spoken word, and either accept or reject it. In respect to a push or a feeling he is not free but merely a thing. The physical selfhood of man is not essentially differentiated from animal selfhood, nor is his psychical selfhood. Man is man primarily in the fact that he hears a voice addressing him from out of eternity. That Truth first makes man a self. Our "I" is grounded in God's "Thou"; it is the answer (*Ant-wort*) to this voice which addresses us. Thou art man as the person addressed, as the second person; and the real meaning of existence, in the midst of the manifest meaninglessness of phenominal existence, can be asserted only by reason of the fact that you accept a meaning which, in contradiction to all experience, you can only receive by faith."

---
[a] *Die Mystik u. das Wort*, p. 97.

Here for the first time we encounter clearly the stress upon the "I" and "Thou" relationship which is characteristic of the Theology of Crisis. It is clearer and more emphatic in quotations which are to follow. I must warn you not to regard it as a peculiarity of this theology. For it is a consideration which is now uppermost in German philosophy. Not the first recognition but the most significant (one might even say, the classical) expression of the fundamental importance of this relationship is Martin Buber's little book of meditations entitled *Ich und Du,* I and Thou. Therefore, when you encounter this thought in what is later to be said, you must not ignore it, nor regard it as a trivial thought, even if it has not hitherto claimed your attention.

I would remark here that in our day the word faith has been discredited, not only for the reason given above (that it must be regarded as superfluous where no "distance" is apprehended) but also because it is a word that has been abused by being confounded with intellectual assent. It is this which provoked both the mystical and the romantic reaction against intellectualism. Yet it did not justify the other and far grosser extreme of confounding faith with feeling and experience. With us, romanticism has degenerated into sentimentalism. The best part of man, we are inclined to think, is below the neck. "In the heart," is the way we like to put it. But physiological psychology rather favors the notion common to the Hebrews and to the Greeks, that the seat of feeling is in "the bowels"—more properly, as we now know, in the solar plexus, the center of the sensory nervous system. But that obliges us to say that the best part of man is below the waist. Or are we not rather compelled to say, in spite of a well founded fear of intellectualism, that reason is at once man's most distinctive and his sublimest faculty? That assuredly we must say, even when we recognize the limitations of reason, or even if we are so absurd as to regard it as an epiphenomenon. It is by this faculty alone we are rendered capable of understanding a *word,* and so of entering into a *personal* relationship with our fellow-men. For it is not by touching our fellow-men that we come into personal relationship with them— not by a blow, and not even by an embrace, if it be only that. And with God whom we cannot touch, how shall we come into personal relationship, unless it be by the reason, Logos, the Word? Personally God touches us, he embraces us in his arms, when he says, "Thy sins are forgiven thee," and nothing brings us so close to God as our acceptance of that incredible Gospel.

It is at this point the Barthian polemic against Schleiermacher and the theology of religious experience first inserts itself. But it is even more trenchant at that point where Christ is regarded as an experience; and it must suffice to introduce it under the next topic, where we regard Christ as the Word.

Here we may consider the last resort of the romantic reaction against intellectualism. It is the assertion of the value of Irrationalism. The present-day champion of Irrationalism is Rudolf Otto; and because his book *The Idea of the Holy* is available in English and has been widely read, you will understand the point of this example of Barthian criticism which I quote from Brunner.[4] Brunner entitles his

---

[4] *Die Mystik u. das Wort,* p. 5. My own interest in Otto's *Das Heilige* was plainly enough shown by the fact that as agent of the Italian Christian Student Federation I had it published in Italy. But from that fact one might hardly guess how dialectical my interest in it is. The study of the religions of mankind had long been my most entrancing and most disquieting occupation. I wondered that

book *Mysticism and the Word*. But his theme is really an alternative: Mysticism *or* the Word. He has Otto expressly in view when he says that "the irrationality of feeling is confounded with the paradox of faith. . . . God comes to us in that he *speaks*. The deeds of God are pro-*clam*ations, Evangelia. *This* is the presence of the 'numinous,' that his thoughts are made known. *This* is the *mysterium tremendum*, that he calls to us, 'Adam, where art thou?' This is the Irrational, that 'the secret which was hid from the creation of the world is now revealed,' that the eternal Truth enters into time, that the reason of all reasons, the truth of all truths speaks, addresses us, and thereby 'calls into being' the truth of man. To hear this call, to give credence to this inapprehensible speech, this Truth which disqualifies all our truth, to recognize it as the guarantee of every truth, to believe this most remote and transcendental truth as applying precisely to *us* and constituting therefore our inmost nature—this is the only participation in God about which the evangelical way of thinking knows anything or is willing to know, because only in this conception is God's sovereignty preserved and the simple reality of man's relation to God truly stated."

You will not be surprised to learn that the theo-

St. Paul could reflect upon "the Gods many and the Lords many" without the uneasy suspicion which haunts our generation that *his* Lord was only one of the many, and that the superiority of Christianity as a religion could only be relative. Otto relieved me of this disquietude. By summing up the prominent aspects of all religions in one picture, he made it abundantly evident how human a thing religion is, how all-too-human, and that for this reason it is identical in all its cults (not excluding Christianity) and substantially indifferent to the names or even to the character of the deities it worships—in short, how religious a thing religion is, and how absolutely it is *not* revelation.

logians we are here dealing with embrace wholeheartedly the Johannine conception of Christ as the Word (Logos) and the Truth. This conception is prominent enough in St. John's Epistles, but in his Gospel it is so prominent that it determines the whole form of the book. I know very well that, to St. John's mind, "truth" implies *reality,* the most substantial reality; but it means reality in the form of truth. And this conception is applied also to the Spirit, who is "the Spirit of truth." And when we note this peculiar emphasis in St. John we must not forget that St. Paul had substantially the same conception of Christ as the revelation of God.

The thought of Christ as the revealing Word is so prominent in the Barthian theology that there might seem to be scant need of any other revelation. This emphasis might have given color to the charge that Barth was reviving the heresy of Marcion, were it not for his devotion to the Old Testament. In fact it is not a singularity of this theology to regard revelation in the Old Testament as pointing to Christ and concentrating upon him, or to think of all subsequent revelation as radiating from that point and concentrating upon Christ's return. The break with orthodoxy is rather to be found in the assertion that Christ is more important than the Scriptures. Brunner says, "People commonly do not believe in the Bible because it testifies to Christ, but in Christ because the sacred books require it." In fact, we should not have a compelling interest to search the Scriptures either of the Old or the New Testament, if we were not convinced that these are they that testify of Christ. In order to maintain that the Old Testament was prophetic of Christ, we are not obliged to handle the Word of God deceitfully and point to the punctual fulfillment of individual prophecies; for it is enough to apprehend that the whole book was a testimony of man's need, and hence an anxious looking forward. The Law prophesied as well as the Prophets. And prophecies which were wide of the mark were none the less veridical prophecies that God would intervene to save his people. In so far as the New Testament is a prophetical book, it may be doubted whether the lines concentrate more surely than did the older prophecies upon the event of the coming Christ, and "whether when the Son of Man comes he will find faith (credence) on the earth."

But the Critical Theology is far from confining its interest to predictive prophecy. It is not even inclined to think of that as the most specific or the most important form of revelation. One thing it is very definite about, that wherever revelation may be detected, it must be regarded as *revelation,* a line falling perpendicularly from above, and not an emanation from the plane on which we find ourselves, or from some place below it. "Revelation" denominates a Word of God in its original form; we know it in its secondary form as the written Word, and in its third form as preaching. This mediation of the Word may be described by a *horizontal* line. But we must remember that wherever the Word of God comes to a man, by whatsoever mediation, he can only hear it as God's Word spoken directly to him, perpendicularly from above. God has spoken in time past unto the fathers, and he still speaks. Therefore Jesus, the unique Word, is not the only Word of God. If before 1 to 30 A. D. God had never spoken, and if he did not still speak, we should hardly be inclined to believe that he then spoke in a unique way in his Son.

It is only as the Word that Christ can be contemporary with us. Albert Schweitzer remarks upon the disconcerting result of the Liberal study of the "Life of Jesus." The purpose was to bring Jesus near, and all the resources of history and archaeology were exploited to this end. But to our dismay, the more we succeeded in picturing his dress, his physical environment, his spiritual traditions, his human limitations, the more inexorably he receded into a remote epoch of the past, the reign of Tiberius Caesar, and into the remotest corner of the outlying province of Judea. *This* is not the sort of "distance" Barth has in view when he insists that with respect to Christ, as well as with respect to God, we need to "reinstate the distance," since we are prone to be too familiar. Nor does Barth recommend that sort of distance at which we place Christ when we regard him as the "Founder" of our religion. "*Not* as an historical force, not as the originator of an historical series, but as the Word of God to us is Jesus the Christ of faith. The category of the Word is that of contemporaneousness. Only the truth has the 'force' to spring over every barrier of time. He who makes his entrance into the truth, thereby makes his *exit* from time. For truth is true only as it is eternal . . . The conjunction Word-faith implies contemporaneousness with Christ, the autonomy of the individual, 'universal priesthood.'"[5] It is in the very nearness of this present and contemporaneous Christ Barth would insert respecful "distance." Brunner complains that Schleiermacher and his followers (and here you are to say, "This is I") "suppress the spiritual relationship indicated by *truth-knowledge* in favor of the category of *cause and effect.* . . . 'Christ' is here regarded as an historical force, as an *élan vital,* or, to use Schleiermacher's own word, as an 'impulse.' With Christ a new force entered the world of history, a push, as it

---
[5] Brunner, *Die Mystik u. das Wort,* p. 220.
[6] *Op. cit.* p. 211 ff.

were, of a specific intensity and direction; and that gave rise to an historical current which may affect the individual, a field of force under the influence of which he may chance to come. To this field of force he gives an apt name: 'the collective life.' The lapidary formulation of this entirely new conception is as follows: 'We are all conscious of a progressive approach in the Christian life to a state of blessedness which is grounded in a divinely constituted collective life, which counteracts the collective life of sin and consequent unblessedness.' To 'faith' as a temporal process corresponds exactly the temporal force as cause. . . . To psychological 'faith' corresponds the historical 'Christ.' Christ is the first cause, the *proton kinoun* of a quasi-physical process. . . . Instead of a spiritual relationship *towards* Christ (which expresses at once the act of faith and the significance of Christ as the Bible and the Reformation understood it) we have simply a picture of dynamic causality: cause-effect, push—yielding, pressure-impression. . . .

"The consequences which derive from this purely dynamic view Schleiermacher himself has drawn, at least in part. The first is this, that a cause which lies in the past can have effects upon me now only through historical media, and that I can have a direct relation only to the last medium and not to the first cause. . . . If Christ is only an historical force, a *proton kinoun*, the cause of a certain current, I can have only indirectly a relationship to him. . . . The Reformers, on the contrary, maintained with confident faith that the individual has an immediate relationship with Christ, in spite of all historical mediation, just as he has a substantially clear relationship to the Word, in spite of psychological mediation. In neither case is the mediation to be denied, but for faith itself and for the relationship which it constitutes none of these things are taken into account. On the contrary, they are ignored."

Brunner goes on to consider "a second consequence of the dynamical view of the 'Christ-impulse,' namely, that like every other impulse it must grow weaker with time." The initial force is consumed in the work which it accomplishes and the resistance it overcomes —like the ripples produced by throwing a stone into the water. In contradiction to the saying, "Blessed are they that have not seen and yet have believed," we must hold that the effect of Christ upon us is necessarily less, immeasurably less, than upon earlier generations of his disciples. We are hardly better off with an "historical Christ" who is so remote from us than with an "ideal Christ" who is unreal. This is substantially Kierkegaard's protest against "the 18,000 years."

I quote these long passages with the hope of persuading you that the "distance" Barth so sternly insists upon, and the faith in revelation which it implies, bring Christ nearer to us than he is really brought by those who would have us think that he is "felt in the blood and felt along the heart."

Finally, for the sake of giving a more succinct and coherent view of the doctrine of revelation as it is held by the more critical of the dialectical theologians, I will summarize the argument of Rudolph Bultmann's small book entitled *The Conception of Revelation in the New Testament*,[7] and at the end will quote several of the most significant passages.

In order to understand what is to follow, you must

---

[7] *Der Begriff der Offenbarung im Neuen Testament*, Mohr, 1929, in the *Sammlung gemeinverständlicher Vorträge*, which means something like "popular discourses"—but they would hardly be accounted such by *us*.

be prepared to concede that revelation may mean not only communication of knowledge by means of the word, but may be an *event,* in which knowledge is not explicit, but by which I may be put in a new position with respect to myself and to others. As, for example, when a crime reveals to me the abyss of human nature and puts me on guard—against myself as well as against others.

Wherein is the limitation to be seen which implies the necessity of revelation? That is the question which ultimately determines what revelation is. And we must not expect this question to be answered undialectically—as if, for example, we were asked to define such a thing as the boundary between Persia and Afghanistan. For what we are here dealing with is a question about the limitation of our *life.* Hence, like our life, it is full of motion. No static answer is possible, but every answer is in turn a question. As it is a question about our life, the knowledge it seeks can never be a matter of indifference, like *e.g.* the style of women's hairdressing in the age of Pericles; but it is knowledge we must have even if we do not want it, and which indeed we *have* in a sense even when we ignore it. For the fact of the limitation of our life is what gives life movement. We carry our death about with us. Hence the question of revelation qualifies our life deeply, for it arises out of the question of our limitation. And just as we can affirm or deny or ignore this question, so also can we treat the question of revelation. Like all life-questions it can be affirmed or denied only by an act of resolution.

In the ecclesiastical tradition, Protestant as well as Roman Catholic, revelation was defined by its relation to *reason.* In the human reason was seen the limitation which revelation transcends by supplying information which the reason unaided could not attain but which it could perfectly well appropriate when once it was given.

In the age of Rationalism *this* limitation was repudiated, definitely and forever, by the apprehension that information about the universe which reason is capable of understanding it might also eventually discover, and that the actual limitations of our knowledge imply only that we have *not yet* got any further. It is natural that when this limitation was disposed of, which was the only limitation hitherto thought of, men should be inclined for a while to suppose that there was actually no limitation of mankind worthy of serious consideration, and that therefore revelation, in the definite and proper sense of the word, was altogether superfluous. When Rationalism spoke of revelation it conceived of it as "natural revelation"— which is a contradiction in terms, because revelation cannot properly be thought of except as supernatural.

This situation was not essentially changed by the Idealistic-Romantic speculation which conceived of revelation as the eternal substratum of life, which was always waiting to be discovered.

A real conception of revelation seemed to be on the point of emerging when men began to see that life is not primarily an expression of reason, and so came to recognize it as an enigma, and to be aware again of limitation. In contradiction to Rationalism, revelation was described as *the Irrational*. "That is right in so far as it asserts that reason of itself can tell us nothing about what lies on the further side of man's limits in the beyond; but at the same time it is false to equate the Irrational with revelation and to suppose that one is speaking about God when one speaks of the Irrational. In so far as the 'Irrational' is treated as something more than a merely formal and therefore a rational idea, in so far as it is supposed really to indicate the riddle of man's existence, nothing in fact but its enigmatical character is thereby asserted. And to hold such knowledge for knowledge of God is to confuse God with the devil. Nevertheless, this opens up again the possibility of speaking about revelation, inasmuch as the limitation of man is again recognized. But precisely this must remain the determinating consideration in dealing with the idea of the Irrational, that it is a knowledge of limitation, a negation, a having *not;* and this possessing *not* must not suddenly be declared to be a possession. When I perceive that my standpoint is the Irrational, I can reasonably ask about revelation; but I have spoiled all when I pretend that in the Irrational I have the revelation."

"And the situation is not altered when one prefers to supplement the notion of the Irrational by referring to feelings which in view of the enigma of existence are capable of gripping and shaking a man—the feeling of creatureliness, of the numinous, and such like. Even in the numinous it is not God man is conscious of, but himself. And he deceives himself when he declares that the numinous is God—even the terrible shudder it produces is a blissful experience. He is then really interested only about himself and not in what is beyond man. Behind this lurks the Romantic, which identifies the Irrational with the Creative, and derives its conception of the Creative from artistic creation."

"This conception of revelation is trivialized by Liberalism, which combines the Rationalistic, the Idealistic and the Romantic motives, and at the same time eliminates the thought which is characteristic of Romanticism, that revelation is something experienced only in creative activity, and instead of this regards revelation as a thing which is objectively before one's eyes in the world and in history so that it can be definitely ascertained and observed."

"In all these efforts to tell what revelation is— even when they are deformed to meaninglessness— the thought is held fast that by revelation man is brought to himself, to an appreciation of his position which he would not otherwise have, and which at least deserves his serious attention. This insures that man must regard his existence as limited, but limited in a way which qualifies it, which renders it anxious and disturbed, and puts it to the question. And talk about revelation will always in some way or another imply that this limitation is a temporary one, that it can be transcended."

"When we come now to enquire about the idea of revelation in the New Testament we must ask first of all how the limitation of man is here understood. And the immediate answer is simply: *Man is limited by death,* the last and the most real enemy (1 Cor. 15:26). Hence the further answer also is simple: *Revelation gives life.*

"What doth it profit a man to gain the whole world and forfeit his life? For what should a man give in exchange for his life" (Mark 8:36 f).

"Wretched man that I am! who shall deliver me out of the body of this death?" (Rom. 7:24).

"To attain salvation is 'to enter into life' (Mark 9:43, 45 *etc.*) or 'to inherit life' (Mark 10:17 *etc.*). The right way is that which 'leadeth unto life' (Mat. 7:14). And that life is revealed is precisely what the Christian message proclaims: 'And the life was manifested, and we have seen and bear witness and declare also unto you the eternal life which was with the Father and was manifested unto us' (I John 1:2). The Christian preaching is 'the word of life' (Phil. 2:16) or 'the words of this life' (Acts 5:20), which is 'according to the hope of eternal life' (Titus 1:2). One repents unto life (Acts 11:18), believes unto life (1 Tim. 1:16), is called unto life (1 Tim. 6:12). For God is he who raiseth the dead (2 Cor. 1:9; Rom. 4:17), and Christ Jesus it is who 'abolished death and brought life and incorruption to light through the Gospel' (2 Tim. 1:10); he is the Prince of life (Acts 3:15). He is the bread of life, the light of life, the resurrection and the life; he who believes on him and follows him has life (John 6:48, 8:12, 11:25, 14:6, 3:15 f *etc.*). As through Adam death came into the world, so through Christ came life (Rom. 5:12-21). Once the end of all our labor was death, now it is life (Rom. 6:21-23; cp. 7:7—8:2 and Gal. 6:8). If in this life only we had set our hope upon Christ, we should be of all men most pitiable (1 Cor. 15:19); but thanks be to God who hath given us the victory through Jesus Christ our Lord, so that it can be said, 'Death is swallowed up in victory! O grave, where is thy victory? O death, where is thy sting?' (1 Cor. 15:55, 57). The Either-Or before which the sermon brings us is death or life (2 Cor. 2:16; 3:6).

"*So death is conceived of absolutely as the barrier before which man stands,* and that not merely in the sense that with this his life is at an end, but rather as the perturbation of our whole life. If it is really the last end, then our whole life is meaningless (1 Cor. 15:32). Our personal existence rises in rebellion against this and knows that with man's proper self it does not comport that he should be subject unto death. But he has no possibility of mastering death. Death is not here, as in the Stoa, treated as a problem which can be disposed of by showing that it does not really concern us, and that one can therefore be master of it by an inward attitude, and in peace of mind attain an ideal immortality. Rather, it does indeed concern us, and we can by no means be master of it. So therefore it was not an *idea* of life that was revealed, which one might appropriate intellectually—not even if such an idea were to pervade the whole of one's life. The only thing revelation can mean is the abolition of death. For what else could it be? An extraordinary knowledge about the world and God? But in death what profit is there to me in all that I know? Creative accomplishment? All that falls victim to death, and I first of all. Experiences? They do not deliver me from death. The numinous? Yes, what is that indeed but death itself? Revelation can only be the gift of life which overcomes death.

"This meaning of revelation is indeed easy to understand. But the New Testament does not say merely that such a revelation must be, but also that it actually is. But how? Revelation is an *act* which destroys death, not a doctrine that there is no such thing. It is an act, however, which is not accomplished *within* human life, but *inwardly from without,* and hence is not recognizable within this present life. *'Eternal life' is no phenomenon of this life*. It consists neither in immortality—for Christians also die—nor in spirituality or inwardness. It can be perceived neither by the eyes, nor by an inner consciousness or feeling. One can only believe in it. It will be authenticated in the resurrection of the dead—that is to say, it is future, and we possess it in hope." But is it to be thought of as the accomplishment of what this present life already is and promises? Clearly not that, for in a certain sense eternal life is already present; it is already actuality through the resurrection of Christ. Death is already conquered. In a certain sense believers are already dead and hence already alive."

Revelation is not communication of knowledge but

an event. It is not a cosmical event outside of us about which the Word gives us information; but it must be an event which intimately concerns us and eventuates in us, in such wise that the Word belongs essentially to it. Preaching itself *is* revelation and does not merely tell of it—in such a way that a man might think that he "has" the revelation when he understands its content. In the very act of giving information the sermon addresses the hearer personally and appeals to his conscience; and he who eludes this address does not understand the information.

The Word of God which is the vehicle of such a revelation is instantly applicable to us and perfectly contemporaneous because, even if uttered in the past, its bearing is eschatological.

This imperfect summary may not suffice to convince you that "the idea of revelation in the New Testament" is here fairly expounded. But there can be no doubt that it is Bultmann's view, and I confess that it indicates the direction in which I look for the solution of this important question. This is obviously the way Paul and John regarded the revelation of Jesus Christ, or at least what they most prized in it. The passages quoted above are enough to prove this—in spite of the fact that in the New Testament one could cull here and there expressions which might indicate a different view of revelation. In Bultmann I can detect a man who, in Unamuno's phrase, is a great *agonizer* with death. But like Unamuno, and to a certain degree unlike Barth, he thinks predominantly of the life which lies beyond death.

LECTURE VII

SALVATION

The last chapter of this book will be devoted to Barth's favorite theme, the preacher and his sermon, as the "third form" of the divine Word. Hence the chapter which here commences is the only place available for the discussion of all the topics of theology which have not been dealt with in preceding chapters. But of course it will not be expected that *all* of them will be considered in the compass of a book which pretends to do no more than call attention to the characteristic aspects of the Theology of Crisis. When we note that in the first volume of his *Dogmatics* Barth has fully discussed and decisively affirmed the traditional doctrine of the Trinity, we need say no more about it here. This is evidently not a point where the Barthian theology is different and distinctive. One of Gogarten's more considerable books is entitled significantly, *I Believe in the Triune God.* We may be consoled by that fact—or else enraged.[1] At all events we know where we stand. In this same volume Barth has handled the doctrine of the Holy

---

[1] Prof. Pauck (*Karl Barth*, p. 189) is so much enraged at Barth for maintaining the doctrine of the Trinity that he exclaims petulantly, "But—God be thanked—the common Christian layman is not a professional theologian," *i.e.* "not concerned with the thought-forms of the past." To which I would remark only that this is a strange thing to thank God for—considering that it is only the layman's ignorance, the fact that he is not a theologian, which saves him from being concerned about the problems stated in the doctrine of the Trinity.

Ghost. And again it is significant that he has chosen the title *Come Creator Spirit* for the collection of sermons which he and Thurneysen issued in partnership. It might seem as if in the Barthian scheme, with its emphasis upon the "distance" and its scepticism in the face of man's claim to sanctification, there were no place for the Holy Spirit. Certainly here too Barth would enjoin a "respectful" distance. But a place there *is* for the Holy Spirit, just as there is a place for the unknown God. It is in a way characteristic of the Barthian theology that in this volume, *i.e.* under the category of the Word, not only the Son is included, but the Father and the Holy Spirit. But this is clearly Johannine theology: the unknown God is revealed in the Word; and "the Spirit of truth" remains to "bear witness" of the Word and "teach all things."

The Church is a topic which Barth has not developed positively. It is hardly yet the time for it. This is still a theme for "marginal notes" and a "theology of correction." For the Church is deeply involved with man's problematical piety, his equivocal cults, and his questionable pretention to holiness. For Barth, the one thing that is not problematical, the one subject that is not treated dialectically, is sin. Anthropology! No need of revelation for what lies so openly before our eyes! Human nature is a theme which is woven in every discussion of Barth's, and he protests that human nature remains human nature, sinful nature, even *after* a man is justified, even in the "saints." Sin is something more than distance between creature and Creator. It is a positive stumbling-block between God and man—an obstacle even for God, and hence *must* be got out of the way. The "distance" means generally the respectful distance a servant must observe in relation to his master; but sin

means the distance of a disobedient servant. It is by
no means necessary to the condition of a servant that
he should be disobedient. It is by no means necessarily characteristic of a creature that he should be in
rebellion against his Creator. Man's sinfulness does
not consist in the fact that he is a creature and as
such is at a distance from his Creator. It consists
rather in the fact that he ignores this distance with
the guilty ambition to be like God. It was not God
that made man what he *is*—what with or without a
special knowledge of anthropology we can so plainly
see him to be—but man, being made in the image of
God, *fell*. Barth has much to say about the Fall—
but nothing about "original sin." That man is *fallen*
we can plainly see; but the Fall is not an event we
can point to in history, it belongs decidedly to prehistory, *Urgeschichte,* in a metaphysical sense—though
Barth is chary of using the word metaphysics because
of a fear that he might be entangled in the conception
of the Idealistic philosophy.

Sin is a proper subject for a chapter entitled Salvation. For how can we speak at all of salvation except
as salvation from sin? Salvation from death, you
may say, and rightly. But what is death but the
punishment of sin? *That* is another fact of anthropology, interpret it as you will. You may prefer to
think, as the romanticists did, of the innocence of
primitive man before his conscience was made uneasy
by the Law—"nevertheless death reigned from Adam
to Moses" (Rom. 5:15). Or more likely you will
prefer to think with the Darwinians that it was creditable to primitive man that he "fell up"—nevertheless
death reigned. And you may think that in the process
of "working out the beast" some men at least have
fallen so high up that they are not properly sinners,
especially if they are pew-holders in the Church—

nevertheless death reigns. And how can it be interpreted except as the clearest possible demonstration that with man God is not well pleased?

Repentence follows sin—or does *not* follow it. Here we are no longer unambiguously on the ground of anthropology. For grace, which is contradictory to sin, is entirely on another plane, and repentence is precariously in between, as the critical Moment of decision between life and death, the decision by which man comes to himself—or else does not. Faith is the name of this decision when it is the choice of life. We have seen how reluctant Barth is to define faith as a *positive* thing, in so far as it is man's act and not God's faithfulness. His scruple is justified by the history of Christian thought. It has been hardly possible for us not to think of our faith as a meritorious distinction. Hence it is wholesome for us to hear that faith is only a vacuum, which God fills. Or with less exaggeration, that it is a leap into the void, the expression of our *desperatio fiducialis*, a "comforted despair." Faith which is sure of itself and confident of possessing something is not faith in God who raiseth the dead. It is not an exaggeration but only a paradox to say that true faith is founded upon doubt and remains always discomforted by it and always agitated. That, therefore, instead of putting our hearts at rest, faith is our perpetual agitator and spur. On the *other* side is God, and God's sure calling in Christ Jesus, grace and election. Yes, Barth talks of election; but he does not understand it like Calvin of particular election. Of course he talks about justification, and he understands it just as the Reformers did —only, in view of the scruple we have been considering, he prefers not to say "justification *by faith*." He would have it understood altogether as God's act, as a *justificatio impii*, a justification of *sinners*—who also remain sinners *after* they are justified and so long as they are in the flesh. "As against God we are always in the wrong," is a saying of Kierkegaard's. The tension here is between man's righteousness and God's righteousness. But if God, the sovereign Judge, pronounces that we are righteous when we are unrighteous, that means that we have become what we are not. Though phenominally we remain sinners, so that no one can unequivocably detect the change; yet "existentially" we are transformed—that is to say, we are put in a new relation to the fundamental terms of our existence, we are really translated into the kingdom of God's dear Son, although our life is still *hid* with Christ in God.—But then what becomes of the doctrine of sanctification?

Before we come to that question it will be well for us to consider what, according to the Theology of Crisis, is *not* the way of salvation. And before *that* let us consider for a moment how a theology like this we are here dealing with must be expounded. I have already insisted that a dialectical theology must be expounded dialectically. But now I have in view the fact that the theology we are here studying is a theology which deals with a few great and concordant ideas, which have the tendency to swallow up many of the individual ideas with which we have become familiar in theology—such, *e.g.* as those I have been briefly considering above. Would it be a fair exposition of this theology, would it be really illuminating, if one were to break up this synthesis and consider each individual topic in its separateness. I have tried not to do that. I am mindful of my early wrestling with the theology of the Johannine writings, which present an analogous case. I am not at all satisfied with my *Doctrine of St. John* written thirty-three years ago, but at least it did not press St. John's thought into a foreign mould. But here we have reached a place where, as I know full well, it is not possible for me to do justice to Barth's thought. We have reached the stone of stumbling, the great scandal of his theology. I am fearful lest he may not do himself justice when in his *Dogmatics* he reaches the point where he must state in a more orderly and systematic way what in his commentary upon the agitated dialectic of St. Paul he has said so confusedly, but so eloquently and so tellingly, about religion—its limitations, its necessity, its meaning and its actuality. How can this be said positively, when it is all so negative? Yet how can the most positive theologian forbear to say it, seeing that it is evidently so necessary to say what is *not* the way of salvation?

The Law is *not* the way of salvation. This is a truth with which we are perfectly familiar—and to which we are heartily indifferent. We must suppose that it was important for the Jews to hear this, since it is the theme which occupies the largest room in two of St. Paul's Epistles—that which he wrote to the Romans, and that to the Galatians. But to us it can have only an archaeological interest. *We* have never been so deluded as to suppose that the ritual precepts of the Mosaic Law indicate the way of salvation; or perhaps even inclined to think that the pious observances which it prescribes were ever meritorious and well pleasing to God. Suddenly Barth made this old Word of God contemporaneous and pungently applicable to us when he interpreted the Law as *religion*. That was an unforgivable offense in the eyes of the historical-critical commentators. And the outcome of it was exceedingly distasteful to all pious people, forasmuch as it implied that what Jesus said against the Pharisees and what St. Paul said against the Law is all of it applicable to us who have the same "zeal for

God" and are as confident as the Pharisees in the efficacy of devout observances. That made it impossible for us to read the old Scriptures in the fifth, sixth and seventh chapters of Romans without finding ourselves obliged to say, "This is I." It turned this harmless protest against putting confidence in the Law into a diatribe against religion—against *our* religion. That was certainly a bold stroke. And yet as we read the commentary we feel no shock at the place where this strange interpretation first emerges. The edge of the wedge is so thin that we hardly observe it. All seems natural at first. And indeed even when we have become alert to the danger we find no place where we can say absolutely, "This is *not* what Paul meant." For what, after all, did the Jews' confidence in the Law mean but the conviction that by devout observances, by the religious dispositions of the heart, and by ethical conduct they were deserving of God's favor? And what else do we mean? There is only one difference. The Jews thought they had good reason to believe that the observances they practiced were prescribed by God and that even the rubrics of their prayer book (indeed chiefly the rubrics!) were written by his hand. But we, without so good a reason, are just as unshaken in our belief that the rubrics of our religion must be well pleasing to God. And how many there are among us who, like the Pharisees, conceive of no other possibility of salvation except the way of religion, that is, by the pious intentions of the heart, by devout observances and by good works. Barth is no more thoroughly convinced than I am that St. Paul repudiated this way of salvation. But taught by experience that my own words are not efficacious in convincing people that this view is even worthy of serious attention,[2] I use only Barth's words in this place, quoting from his *Romans*. It will be seen that he criticises religion as only a religious man can criticise it, that he does not simply decry it as a mere human possibility (which as such is no possibility beyond the "death line" where salvation is sought), but also recognizes it as a human necessity, and as man's highest possible possibility, the very apex of his attainment.

"The Law worketh death." "Is the Law sin?" St. Paul then asks; and he answers, "God forbid!" Again he asserts, "The Law is holy, and the commandment is holy, righteous and good." To this says Barth: "What shall we do? asks the man who under the fearful pressure of his position as a man in the world has come to himself and to the consciousness of what is required of him and of his distance from God, and so has become a religious man. And the answer to this question can only be, Above all keep asking! God maintain for us this question! May it as a question encircle us on all sides, rob us of all answers which are not themselves questions, cut off every way of escape, every easy evasion! . . . Within the bounds of humanity religion is doubtless the *holy*, pointing away from the human and towards the divine; it is *righteousness*, the corrolary, the parallel, the parable of the divine will; it is the good, the procedure and the situation which in the mediateness of our relation to God testifies (if that be possible) to the lost immediateness. The wish to shun it because we are consciously or unconsciously aware how equivocal and dangerous it is, *either* leads us back to other

---

[2] My book *Religion or Faith* seems to have persuaded nobody that the possibility of such an antithesis can be entertained by one who is not an enemy of Jesus Christ, and when in *Jesus According to St. Mark* I point my finger at the evident instances in which Jesus decries religion, it has been regarded as blasphemy.

deeper seated human possibilities, perhaps to the ethical, logical, or aesthetical, or perhaps even deeper —*or else* sideways to old or newer religious variants, which, in case the variator should not be thoroughly aware of the essential limitations of the religious process, are sure to be poorer variants. The cry, Forward! beyond the religious possibility, indicates no human possibility. . . . Would then that we might *be* religious men, in the posture of *adoratores,* watching, waiting and hastening with all our heart and with all our soul and with all our strength! And to arouse religion, to keep it awake and to nourish it, above all however to reform it, rather to revolutionize it again and again, is verily a task, if any task there is, which is worth the sweat of the noble." (P. 236 f.)

At any rate, about the reality of religion there can be no doubt, or about its actuality. "We have represented the new world as standing in victorious opposition to the old. But is there not something here that we have forgotten, overlooked, suppressed? This relationship of man to God in which we are either 'in Adam' or 'in Christ,' has it not also its human, subjective side? Alongside of the invisible possibilities of the 'old' and the 'new' man, is there not also to be taken into account the visible possibility of being a . . . religious man? Between Adam and Christ is there not a third term, namely, Moses with his brother Aaron, the prophet and the priest, the believing, hoping and loving man, god-fearing, consecrated to God, zealous for God, the awakened man, watching, hastening, hearing, seeing, ready and active, daring to leap into the void, or at least faithful in small things, the thinker, or else the executive, or else the man of prayer—in short religion past and present? Where religion is, is not the threshold on which the new man stands already *passed?* Does not a sane and vigorous human divineness and divine humanness serve visibly as *substitute* for the dialectical balance of sin and righteousness? Is not a portion, at least a little bit, of the new world already visibly *given* downright? We take this question very seriously. It is perfectly true that the God-relationship has its subjective, human, historical side. It is a fact that cannot be too much insisted upon that there are religious men, that the religious attitude, religious thought and religiously inspired activity in thousands of different forms (how many of them attractive, earnest, awe-inspiring, strong!) become again and again historical reality. We may criticise relatively the manifold manifestations in the field of religion, and yet we are obliged ever and again to come to a halt with a relative recognition of it. Complaints which apply only to its accidental form and figuration religion is always able to meet. For among all human possibilities religion is actually the most penetrating, the purest, the most vital, the most capable of adaptation. Religion is the human possibility to receive and hold an impression of God's revelation: to portray, record and develop in the visible forms of human consciousness and human creativeness the twisting and turning movement from the old to the new man; the possibility in solitude or in society of adopting an attitude corresponding to the way of God with men, preparing it, or accompanying it, or following it after, and somehow, consciously or unconsciously, giving this attitude concrete expression. . . . But obviously, as a *human* possibility, as an historical manifestation, by reason of the fact that it is entirely interwoven with the world of men, that its assumed divine content is entirely concealed by phychical, intellectual, moral and sociological form, it is simply old world and stands in the shadow of sin and of death." (P. 162 f.)

Perhaps there is no better recommendation of religion than this which follows: "The reality of religion is conflict and offense, sin and death, the devil and hell. It by no means leads men out of the problematic of guilt and destiny, but squarely into it. It gives him no solution of his life's problem, but rather makes him an insoluble enigma to himself. It is neither his salvation, nor a discovery of it; it is rather the discovery that he is not saved. It is neither to be enjoyed nor acclaimed, but as a hard yoke which cannot be thrown off it is to be borne. Religion is a thing one can wish on no one, or praise, or recommend to another. It is a *misfortune* which falls with fatal necessity upon some men, and from them is carried to others. It is the misfortune under the weight of which John the Baptist goes into the wilderness to preach repentence and the judgment to come; under the weight of which such a deeply moving long-drawn-out sigh as the second Epistle to the Corinthians was put on paper; under the uncanny weight of which a physiognomy like that of Calvin becomes what it finally was. It is the misfortune, however, under which apparently every one has to sigh who is called man." (P. 241.)

St. Paul says, "For the wish is there, but to do what is good is not" (Rom. 7:18). To which Barth remarks: "But what is 'wish'? Surely it is striving, desiring, expecting, seeking, praying, knocking. The last and most promising word of all pastoral preaching, breathlessly repeated, and enhanced ever with new emphasis, variation and reinforcement by all the witnesses of the truth of all times—perhaps so breathlessly just because the sense of it is so terribly simple, and because it is so terribly evident that within the reality of religion this simplicity actually is the last word. If this does not take hold, what will? But indeed it does take hold. The word, '*Seek* God!' will ever find attentive ears, just because it is the last word that human ears are capable of hearing—and certain it is that the number of earnest wishers, honest seekers after God, is vastly greater than it might seem to superficial observation. *Who* can declare of *whom* that he is not an honest wisher? Perhaps I am a God-seeker. 'The wish is present.' " (247.) I follow this with a quotation from Bultmann:[a] "Then the question about the absoluteness of the Christian revelation or the Christian faith cannot any longer be raised. If the question is asked from a point of view outside of faith, with the purpose of establishing a graded valuation of all the religions, including the Christian, regarded as world phenomena, it is meaningless from the first; for in the purview of such a question everything is relative and nothing absolute. The question can be meaningful only when it is asked from the point of view of faith; but then it is already decided, for faith is simply the answer to revelation. From the point of view of faith, however, the history of religions is meaningful; for faith, because it understands itself, understands the 'religions'—including the 'Christian' religion—as a questioning about God, about revelation, and sees in them that provisional understanding of revelation which one now has begun radically to understand."

What becomes then of our "sanctification"? It is hard to hear our religion disparaged, for that we regard as a chief part of our sanctification. But what will Barth do with the rest of it?—with all the noble sentiments and dispositions upon which we pride ourselves? and the fine qualities which characterize us as Christians in our active life? We can foresee, perhaps, that he will deal hardly with us. For the Law

---
[a] *Der Begriff der Offenbarung*, p. 43.

was a moral as well as a ritual code; and if the sentence "No confidence in the Law!" can properly be applied to our religion, how much more to our morality. St. Paul was no longer thinking about the Law as religion when in the seventh chapter he drew such a sorry picture of his own moral inadequacy; and Barth is thinking only partly of religion when he comments as follows: "We are back again at the same point where we started from at the beginning of the chapter: the religious man is 'a man for so long time as he liveth' (7:1); he is *this* man in *this* world, the humanly possible man whom we all know. *The man who never should be what he is, and never is what he should be. The* man who in his mortal body, which he inseparably and indivisibly is, carries about with him the reminder that he (no other than *he!*) belongs to death. Whither can all our conclusions about the reality of religion properly lead us but to the most fundamental scepticism about the possibility of *this* man? He cannot really live, and he cannot die! Actually, and just because of his piety, he hangs between heaven and earth! But what good does the most radical doubt do me when the one thing certain is that I *am* this man? when no psychical subtleties or dialectical ingenuities can help me over the brutal fact of this 'I am'? when I who by the religious possibility itself am taught to see can see no other possibility but just the possibility of being this man? 'O wretched man that I am!' Do we know now, at last, what man is? and what is the reality of religion? and how very far from this reality of religion was the triumphant note which presided at the cradle of that idea which the spiritual guides of the nineteenth century liked to call religion? The reality of religion is the horror of man at himself.—But *Jesus Christ* is the new man, beyond the possible men, beyond especially all the pious men. He is the abolition of *this* man in his totality. He is the man who has come to life out of *death*. He is—I do not say *me*, but—my existential self, the 'I' which in God and in God's freedom I am." (P. 252.)

You are not to suppose that Barth would go the length of denying that religion is a sanctifying influence, as even historians and psychologists allow. No one can really have a religion without being influenced by it in his disposition and conduct. It is often not difficult to trace to a religious influence fine traits of character and reputable standards of conduct. Yet at the same time scoffers do not suffer us to forget that censoriousness and hypocrisy are also religious dispositions—and we cannot say this without remembering that Jesus was one of the boldest scoffers at religion. Moreover, it is puzzling to note that very different characters may be developed by the same religion. St. Francis of Assisi and St. Ignatius Loyola were both Catholics. It would not be in point here to contrast with either of them representative Protestants, since Protestantism might be regarded as a different religion. But it adds to our perplexity to observe on the other hand that religions which are totally different may produce similar characters. St. Francis is not a precise match for the Hindu Ghandi, but there are saints in the Church calendar who are. To add to our perplexity, we are obliged to recognize that atheism also has its saints. In the Positivism of Comte there is a decided strain of puritanism, and there is more of it in soviet Russia than in the New England of today. It is all very confusing! Even the phenomena of conversion, as they are now studied by psychologists, are seen to be very human, and not referable exclusively to religious impressions. Our "sanctification" proves to be at least exceedingly problematical.

Moreover, it is exceedingly relative. All the invidious superiorities which we can boast of as pious men are terribly relative. Knowing this, St. Paul said, "If I must needs glory, I will glory of the things that concern my weakness." It is very observable in the New Testament that "the glorious company of the Apostles," and indeed the first century Christian fellowship as a whole, showed no inclination to point to themselves as shining examples of Christian virtue, were not accustomed to relate the triumphant experience of their conversion for the edification of others, and still less disposed to suggest that their very visible sanctification combined with their very visible unsanctification was a persuasive vindication of the righteousness of God—not to say the final, conclusive and long lacking proof of God's existence.

But from the point of view of the Theology of Crisis the decisive thing is that all our goodness, though it reach superlative heights, is utterly irrelevant to the life which shall be—if we have in view the *qualitative* difference of the kingdom of God, where "they neither marry nor are given in marriage, but are like the angels in heaven." Our goodness here can seem relevant to the life there only in case we soar triumphantly over the fact of death and conceive that we simply "pass" into the other world, which is not qualitatively a different world but only a new stage in our continuous progress. A conception which is plainly implied by the prayers for the dead with which we have recently enriched the Prayer Book. They speak of "continual growth," of service here, of course, but also of "service" there, with the only difference that there it will be "perfect." A conception which is clearly more American than Biblical.

From this point of view it must seem exceedingly necessary that we commence to refine our souls here, and it can reasonably be expected (although no such condition is suggested in the Bible!) that only finely fibred souls can inherit the kingdom of God. But if it is a question, not of the immortality of the soul, but of the resurrection of the dead, then (however much we may dislike it) we must regard all our goodness as "interim ethics," and it cannot seem incredible that the dying thief, with all his imperfections on his head, should receive the promise, "Today shalt thou be with me in paradise." Incredible, yes! but not *more* incredible than when that assurance is given to us.

You must remember that I am speaking as an expositor of the Theology of Crisis. For I would not have it suspected that in my own person I should be inclined to speak disparagingly of religious piety—especially at a time when there is so deplorably little of it. *This* is the place where Barth feels it necessary to assert that "a Christianity which is not altogether and utterly eschatological has altogether and utterly nothing to do with Jesus Christ." It is this which calls a Halt! to our boasting about sanctification. Proleptically we are sanctified, we are redeemed, we are glorified. We must be content to *hope* for our salvation, hoping against hope, and judging in despite of all experiences. For as yet "our life is *hid* with Christ in God." Our baptism is a "baptism *unto* the remission of sins." The bread which we break is a *pledge* of eternal life, looking forward to "that day" —*Maranatha! Now* we do well to glory only in our weaknesses; but even now we can "glory in the hope of the glory of God" (Rom. 5:2).

It is true, the early Christians spoke of *one another* as "saints"; but the phrase "called to be saints" sufficiently explains what they meant. They talked (infrequently) about "sanctification." But sanctification properly means much more than moral goodness—and much less. It means holiness. It is applied to things as well as to persons. It is a quality which belongs to God first of all—and to persons and things which are appropriated to him. It means that God has claimed us, has laid his hand upon us (Gogarten), with all the comforting implications of such a thought —and all discomforting obligations.

We have to give up all thought of meritorious sanctification, if we are to preserve (or recover) the *distinctive* character of Christianity. For Christianity is not distinguished from the other great religions of the world by the fact that it is a religion of salvation, but by the fact that it alone proclaims sheer forgiveness, that is to say, a *justificatio impii*. No other religion, no mere religion, ever has had the boldness to conceive that God might forgive sinners simply as sinners who have no other recommendation but simply repentence and the tragic "wish" to be good. In our hearts we do not desire to believe such a thing, unless we are in despair about ourselves. A salvation which God and God alone purposes and plans and carries through is distasteful to all men who have a sense of human dignity, for it would evidently be more noble if we should coöperate—if we could claim at least some moral distinction to justify beforehand God's justification of us, or triumphantly to vindicate it afterwards. We have in fact lost sight of this chief distinction of Christianity, and are therefore left to wonder why, in the conflict of religions during the second century, the Church was so bitterly hated by the wise and good, and yet prevailed. Origen[4] quotes the best informed and most redoutable opponent of

---

[4] *Against Celsus*, Bk. III, Cap. 59.

Christianity as saying: "Those who invite to participation in other mysteries make proclamation as follows: 'Every one who has clean hands and a prudent tongue'; others again: 'He who is pure from all pollution, whose soul is conscious of no guilt, who has lived well and justly.' Such is the proclamation of those who promise purification of sins. But let us hear what kind of persons these [Christians] invite. Everyone, they say, who is a sinner and is devoid of understanding, is a child, and in fine is in the clutch of the devil (*kakodaimon*), him will the kingdom of God receive. And what do you mean by a sinner, if not an unjust person and a thief, a house-breaker and a poisoner, a perpetrator of sacrilege and a robber of the dead? What other sort of people would a man invite if he were summoning a council of robbers?"

Celsus here, besides giving precious information to the archaeologists about the proclamations of the mystery cults, puts his finger precisely upon the distinction of Christianity, showing that the Church did not encounter such cut-throat competition as we have supposed, but had a monopoly in its line of business, being the only religion which addressed itself to sinners. That is to say, it is not a religion among others, but the revelation of the incredible goodness of God. If we do not preserve this distinction of the Church as the Church for sinners, we are no longer exponents of Christianity, though we may cling to the name. This same Celsus, remarking upon the heretical sects of Christianity, shrewdly observed that the one thing they had in common with the Church, the one thing they were ashamed to give up, was the *name* of Christian.

Only as we give God all the glory, exalting the fact of his justification of us and checking the pretense that we are worthy, is the atonement of the Cross illuminated for us with a full light, against the total obscurity of that side which is turned towards God. "Golgotha was the end of the Law, the boundary of religion. . . . As seen from the Cross, religion as a given fact of psychology and history, as the visible comportment of men thus and so, has been 'taken out of the way' (Col. 2:14). A man stands before God, not as a 'religious' man, any more than in the confidence of any other human capacity, but in the *divine* capacity in which Christ stood before God in *that* hour when his 'religious consciousness' was the consciousness of God's desertion of him. From thence—from the non-being of man (and particularly of religious men!) which becomes visible in the slain body of Christ—is visible the Atonement, Forgiveness, Justification, Redemption" (Barth, *Rom.* p. 216).

LECTURE VIII

PREACHERS AND PREACHING

Here and there the topic of preaching has cropped up incidentally in the course of these lectures, and I think it will be felt that everything that has been said here is clearly applicable to the preacher's problem. The Theology of Crisis is preëminently a theology which can be preached. It was wrought out with constant reference to the preacher's need. Primarily it was Barth's own need as a preacher in a small Swiss town which prompted him to write the queries and "marginal notes" which resulted in his *Romans*. And though the success of that book forced him into a chair of theology, he remains absorbed in the preacher's problem, as the first volume of his *Dogmatics* plainly shows. He is himself a powerful preacher, as are several of those who have gathered about him to form a school.

This topic therefore deserves a conspicuous place in any exposition of the Theology of Crisis. It is not a theology of *crisis* except as it actually provokes a crisis, and that is only possible through preaching. In all the books which assay to describe the Barthian theology for English readers this topic has in fact been given a large place. Moreover, it is the topic of two chapters in the one book of Barth's which is available in English—*The Word of God and the Word of Man*. In that book there is one passage which is frequently quoted: "This situation I will characterize in the three following sentences: As ministers we ought to speak about God. We are human, however, and so cannot speak about God. We ought therefore to recognize at the same time our obligation and our disability and by that recognition give God the glory. This is our perplexity."

That this paradox was not lightly uttered is shown by the fact that it is taken up again and elaborated in the *Prolegomena* to the *Dogmatics* (pp. 47-65). He refers there to the first pages of his book, which we quoted in our introductory lecture, and remarks that in this earlier passage he treated phenomenologically the problem of speech about God, whereas now the problem must be dealt with in a different way in view of the fact that speech about God occurs specifically in the form of the sermon, as speech addressed by men to men. That such a thing should be done and can be done is not a matter of course. Barth characterizes it as an "act of daring." And by that he does not mean what we mean when we talk romantically of a "Christian adventure." He says explicitly, "An act of daring is an adventure in which one is clearly conscious, or ought to be, that many and weighty reasons speak against the possibility of its succeeding. To say, 'He dares it,' is to use an expression which is evidently too weak to describe the enterprise which theology undertakes. It undertakes something against the success of which all reasons protest." Barth considers first the "difficulty" of knowing God about whom we are to speak, and he concludes that it is an "impossibility." Yet that he reckons not the greatest "difficulty." Preachers claim to have some sort of knowledge of God, although their hearers are likely to be sceptical about it. Assuming that one has such knowledge, that one really knows about God, about the God who is above all

Gods—"how absolutely must he close his mouth! Into what impossible loneliness must he retreat who really knew God and dared to speak about him!— how far from the roads trodden by the many, and even from the quiet paths of the finest and the noblest! Besides—he who speaks about God to others cannot but address them exactingly. He cannot be content that others should let him talk and should listen with interest. He demands the specific and unique attention, gratitude and willingness which is characteristic of the obedience of faith. He wants to bring men before God, to claim them for God's service, to win and save their souls, to take possession of them for the kingdom of God." Considering all that this implies, and the resistance which it is bound to meet on the part of men, Barth concludes, "How can one muster up courage for such a task?" "But assuming finally that I have not only knowledge of God but somehow have courage to speak about him, the third and most difficult question remains, What right have I actually to do such a thing? The tacit judgment of the world about theologians—and most of all against the more learned of them and the more courageous— is unanimous to the effect that their business is a tactless intrusion and presumption. They ask who has appointed us warders and stewards of the sanctuary? Have we reasons weighty enough for ignoring the respectful silence about the highest and the most intimate affairs which most men, perhaps not only out of godlessness, are accustomed to observe, while we on the other hand are constantly breaking it with crude words, turning unasked our insides out, and prying unasked into the inmost parts of others? They wonder if we really believe seriously in our authorization to preach to them faith and repentence and to exact it. Or are we not officious meddlers and adventurers whom one has a good right to ward off? One cannot too thoroughly place himself under the Damocles sword of these questions before and while others place him there. As against them are we content to appeal to the fact of our theological education? Or perhaps rather to occurrences in our life, to illuminations and experiences which we can refer to in our past? It is to be hoped that such appeals will be cut short before they cross our lips by insight into the entire incongruousness between that which we say and that which we do, by perception of the judgment in which we stand for the fact that we are always speaking of that which is too high for us. The appeal to the fact of our ecclesiastical ordination rests in any case upon presumptions to the knowledge of which the perception that we are actually unqualified should not only once but ever again be the beginning. Thinking existentially, we must not only disclaim the knowledge and the courage to speak about God, but the right also to do it."

So the preacher's task is "impossible!"—unless and except "it might be that the theologian, in spite of the recognized impossibility, nevertheless preaches because he *must*, and must preach because he is under orders. If there *is* a Word of God, and if the business of preaching has something to do with it, finds its origin and its aim in it, then would there be given a possibility of speaking about God which would in no wise signify an atenuation of the impossibility we have been considering." "The daringness of the sermon would then be qualified as obedience, coming under the sign of the highest responsibility and promise; but it would not cease to be daring, and a daring of the impossible." The lack of knowledge of God would be qualified as obedient *docta ignorantia.* And the courage to dare it would be rather the lack of courage not to do what is enjoined.

Having reached this point where it is understood that the sermon deals with the Word of God, Barth observes that "the Word of God, the correlate and reflex of which in the sermon are human words, is itself properly *word,* speech of reason to reason, logos, which rests upon knowledge and expects understanding; it indicates the relationship with which revelation has to do, a relationship between two, by which these two are unequivocally indicated as I and Thou, as two persons. Hence the preacher is not commissioned to lisp, to mimic, to make music, because the Word of God which he is commissioned to preach and which alone makes it possible for him to be a preacher is itself speech." More important it is to observe that God is always the subject of his Word. " 'God's Word'—this conception is always equivalent to 'God speaks,' whether we have in mind revelation, or the Scriptures, or the preaching of the Church. . . . There exists in the Bible no petrified or in any other wise conserved Word of God independent of God's action as the speaker. God spoke, and he still speaks in the words of the preacher, in spite of the fact that these are human and imperfect words. There would be no hope for the Church, if it were only through wise and right words of genuine preachers God could speak to his people. And the position of the preacher would be hopeless, if he felt that God could not make himself heard in the foolishness of his preaching. "It was appropriate that medieval painters used as symbol of the Madonna a clear crystal vase. The Logos seeks such vessels—seeks to make our speech about God into such transparent vessels. It is *not* said, even in the case of the purest doctrine, that God will actually accept it and speak through it when we speak.

It is grace when he does so. It is not said that he cannot speak through the medium of very impure doctrine. The Church would be lost, if in this respect God were not ever and again gracious to her. But this freedom and grace of God does not alter the fact that this task as such is prescribed to us. When we have done all that it was our duty to do, then shall we say, We are unprofitable servants. But whoever would conclude from this that we might just as well be lazy servants only shows that he knows not what he says" (p. 420).

With this agrees substantially Bultmann's view of God's activity in the sermon. In the fourth lecture we saw that he conceives of revelation as an *act* of God. God still acts, and he acts in the sermon. It is not merely an act of the past which the sermon brings near to us in the fact of recounting it and giving information about it, but God's act is made contemporaneous in a much more actual sense, being performed in the present and in my presence. For the hearer there is no way that leads behind the sermon, were it to an "historical Jesus," or to a cosmical event which once upon a time happened somewhere. Rather everything that is essential happens in his presence: "Now is the day of salvation." In the present and contemporary Word revelation "finds" a man, and thereby accomplishes itself upon him, whether he will hear or whether he will forbear. Believers and unbelievers as well are by that act qualified; the decision is made, whether for life or for death.

All this is clear enough, yet it may be a disappointment to find that Barth and his colleagues have nothing to say about *how* the sermon is to be composed and preached—about all the questions with which homiletics ordinarily deals. You may wonder that they are so agonizingly concerned with a problem which perhaps has not occurred to us as a problem at all. Though we might well be reminded of it by the first words which are written in the order for Morning Prayer: "The Lord is in his holy temple, let all the earth keep silence before him"; or by St. James' warning: "Be not many teachers, knowing that ye shall receive heavier judgment." The problem which commonly concerns us is how to make the sermon interesting to the hearers, so that they will come willingly and come again. Barth is not altogether silent on that subject. He considers very seriously what motive it is which brings people again and again to the Church in spite of continual disappointment. It is the craving to hear something about God and the last things, about life and death, or death and life. He pictures eloquently their vague craving, and the disappointment they are only half aware of when they go away after hearing an interesting discourse about this or that which has nothing to do with their real question—the question they come to put to the priest, and not to the psychologist, the physician, the scientist, the statesman, or the eloquent lecturer upon *omnibus rebus et quibusdam alliis*.

The Barthian concern about the problem of preaching will certainly seem strange to us if we have never even so much as thought that it might be our duty to preach God's Word. Not quite so strange to pastors in Germany, for there the tradition is still preserved that the sermon must start with a text from the Bible and be an exposition of it. This of course was once our custom, but no longer do we feel rigorously bound to observe it. And to me it has seemed a custom more honored in the breach than in the observance, seeing how cavalierly the text is commonly treated, and how soon the preacher is quit of it. But it is more ominous that in our sermons we no longer feel rigorously bound to speak about God. It is still worse when the preacher, remembering tardily that this is properly the subject of Christian preaching, and ashamed to conclude without mentioning him, drags God in unceremoniously by the heels.

It is assumed by Barth as a matter of course that the Christian sermon will be based upon the Christian Scriptures of the Old and New Testament, that the Word of God in its third form will follow and will not supercede the second form which we have in the Bible. If this no longer seems a matter of course to us, it is still well worth considering with a view to investing the preacher's word with the authority it now notoriously lacks. For, amazing as it is, the people in general still believe in the Bible, in spite of the painstaking efforts of a million ministers, Sunday by Sunday, throughout several generations, to convince them that it is not essentially different from any other book. They do not believe that it is inerrant in the account it gives of history and of pre-history, they do not look to it for scientific information, and they are likely to reject in a lump all its reports of miracle because they lack the sagacity to discriminate; but they are very much inclined to believe that the solemn words it contains about God and about man's relation to God do not come from the tip of the tongue and are far more worthy of consideration than anything the preacher has to say when he is frankly expressing his own opinions, or even when he refers to his own experiences. The Bible is still an authority for the people. If they do not read it, or in reading it they discover that they cannot read it with profit, it is because we have taught them that it is unscientific to make its words contemporaneous and apply them personally to themselves. The Bible is still in a position to invest the preacher's words with authority—but only on the condition that his words are evidently conformable with the authority which he cites, that they are the contemporaneous form of the eternal truths which are registered in the Bible. If we were to declare frankly that what we have to say does not express the essential meaning of the Bible but is something better, or if we were solemnly to place upon the lectern another book or books in place of the Bible, the people would leave in a block, or else see to it that we got out. No preacher has ever been known to be so frank—partly for the reason that we cannot bear to be so frank with ourselves. But you cannot fool all the people all the time. In the long run the more discerning will perceive it, if we are handling the Word of God deceitfully, and, in case they still are willing to hear us talk, they will cheerfully acquiesce in our preference to avoid the appeal to Scripture.

It is often suggested that an "expository sermon" might be tried as a change, with the hope of reviving flagging interest. Not infrequently this expedient is tried—and almost always it fails. For the very obvious reason that an expository sermon is intolerable to the preacher and unconvincing to the congregation, if it does not honestly expound what is said in the Bible and meant by it. It can only have the effect of making evident how far our modern Christianity has moved away from its source. That in itself may be salutary. It makes it clear at all events that a preacher who is seriously concerned to bring the people back to a genuine apprehension of Christianity has no other resource but this authority, and that he must use it disingenuously, without employing any "key to the Scriptures," whether it be in the open and reputable way of Christian Science, or clandestinely.

Barth's own example shows with what power an expository sermon can be preached. A Barthian expression which I encountered lately in *Zwischen den Zeiten* revealed to me how tragical a thing clericalism is for the cleric. Here clericalism is understood simply as "giving out more than one has." That fairly depicts our pitiable situation—unless we have (as indeed we have in the Bible) far more than in our own experience and learning we actually have.

As a preacher I have long been haunted by a phrase in Ruskin's precious little book *Unto This Last*. After defining precisely the parts which other professions, more evidently useful, may be expected to play in the world, he defines the duty of our profession: "The duty of the clergyman is to remind people in an eloquent manner of the existence of God." These words at first were bitter to me. But apart from the "eloquent manner," I can find no fault with this definition. It strikes a Barthian note. Barth too would emphatically "remind" us of, and *not* prove, the existence of God. When I reflect how great the need is that people should constantly be reminded of God, and that to remind them is to speak the ineffable word, I see an heroic challenge in this duty, perceive that it is a daring task which I cannot dare to neglect; but however much exalted I may be by the thought of so great an undertaking, I cannot myself forget that nothing more glorious is expected of me but just to "remind people."

www.ingramcontent.com/pod-product-compliance
Lightning Source LLC
Chambersburg PA
CBHW071229170426
43191CB00032B/1195